D1737233

BE A

Glowstick

Girl

A Collaborative Book

by Tina Torres

Dedicated to all the women out

there who have been broken

and now shine bright!

Introduction

Have you ever experienced a moment when you felt completely shattered as if your life had been fragmented into countless pieces with no hope of recovery? It's a sentiment that resonates with many of us at some point in our lives, and it can be an incredibly distressing experience.

However, I want to offer you a different perspective — one that suggests that being broken can be a necessary and transformative process. In fact, by embracing your brokenness, you have the potential to shine even brighter than before. It may sound counterintuitive, but bear with me.

Let's consider the analogy of a glowstick. When you initially remove it from its packaging, it appears to be an ordinary plastic tube. Yet within that seemingly mundane exterior, two chemicals are waiting to be combined. The fusion of these chemicals triggers a chemical reaction, causing the stick to emit a radiant glow in the dark. Paradoxically, for the glowstick to fulfill its purpose and shine, it must first be broken. The stick is no longer intact by snapping it in half and mixing the chemicals, yet it illuminates its surroundings.

Similarly, in life, there are moments when we need to break in order to reach our full potential. Our challenges and struggles serve as catalysts for personal growth and development, enabling us to emerge as stronger, more resilient versions of ourselves. When faced with difficult circumstances, we are compelled to dig deep within ourselves, unearthing hidden reservoirs of strength and resilience that we may not have known existed.

During times of brokenness, we have an incredible opportunity to rebuild ourselves in a way that surpasses our previous state. We can carefully piece together the fragments of our shattered lives, forming a new mosaic that reflects our enhanced resilience and self-awareness. Through this reconstruction, we can become more vibrant and whole, embodying the strength and wisdom we have acquired through our experiences.

However, embracing brokenness is not solely for our own benefit. By harnessing our journey of healing and growth, we become beacons of light for others who may be traversing similar paths of darkness and despair. Our personal transformation and the insights gained from our struggles can serve as guiding lights, offering solace and encouragement to those navigating their own shattered realities. In sharing our stories and providing support, we help others realize that their brokenness does not define them and that there is hope for a brighter tomorrow.

So, if you find yourself in a state of brokenness and despair, please know that it is okay to feel this way. Remember that you are not alone in your experiences and that healing, and restoration is possible. Embrace your brokenness, for within it lies the potential for profound transformation and a renewed sense of purpose. You possess the innate ability to shine brighter than ever, illuminating your path and inspiring others to find their way amidst the darkness.

Forward

— Jessica Higdon —

Life is a roller coaster, filled with ups and downs that can shape who we become. Growing up with a bipolar mother, I experienced the uncertainty of unconditional love and the pain of verbal abuse. When you grow up like that, you never know if you'll be loved and hugged all day or told that you're the biggest piece of garbage that's ever lived. It's quite unstable.

When I was 11 years old, my mom dropped me off at my grandparent's home and planned never to pick me up again. I lived with her full-time while my dad would visit on the weekends; he had no idea what she had been planning.

She was planning to kill herself that day.

Luckily, she didn't succeed and decided to get the help she needed that day. This story has a happy ending. However, it didn't change the fact that until I was an adolescent teenager, I lived in an extremely unstable environment, which shaped my entire character. It was an extremely challenging environment that made me a people pleaser, always seeking validation and unsure of my worth. Would I ever truly be loved?

If you can relate to this in any way (and ladies, I know there are many people pleasers out there), I want you to know that your biggest roadblock can become your biggest asset in life.

Because of my past, I had a strong desire for stability and certainty, which has served me in a BIG way my whole life. I've always been a fast decision-maker and am driven toward creating a security blanket (financially) for my family. When I take a step back and look at everything that happened, I realize that my perspective has grown so much, given my experiences.

I'm a mother now, and I see that she was doing her best with her circumstances. I can understand how being a single mother creates hardships I never understood as an adolescent. I've completely forgiven her for everything I went through, as her heart and intentions were pure.

I refused to let my past define me. Through hard work and the power of social media, at 21 years old, I built a successful six-figure home business income. At 23 years old, we (my husband and I) hit our first million-dollar year and have made multiple seven figures ever since.

However, I soon realized that money alone couldn't fulfill my true passion. I was making amazing money and good at what I did, but there was still a void and an emptiness inside me I didn't understand. I realized I was not living according to what I had been put on this planet to do!

Real estate had always captivated me, and I leaped, diving into the luxury market with my license in hand. It has been the best decision I ever made, even though, at the time, I was VERY nervous to switch careers.

Following your passion can be terrifying, especially when others have certain expectations of you. It's even harder when you're financially tied to something that doesn't bring you joy, like "Golden Handcuffs."

But I discovered God has a plan for us, including joy, love, and serving others. If what you're doing doesn't bring you joy, it may be time to reconsider your path.

I've had massive success and made major downs shifts throughout my life, relying on faith to guide me. When I trust God's path, I've never been steered wrong.

In this book, I am honored to share my journey alongside some of the smartest and most talented women I know. Their wisdom and guidance will inspire you to take action and implement the instructions given. Let this not be just another book on your shelf but a catalyst for change and growth.

I'll end with this...

Last year, my mom passed away. As I was taking care of her and stroking her hair, I had this inclination that it was getting close to the end. Suddenly, I had an overwhelming feeling of forgiveness and love come over me, and I understood everything I had gone through and why. I completely broke down in tears.

You can call this whatever you'd like, but I know in my heart something divine was trying to tell me that what seems like our biggest struggles at the time actually work for our good in ways we can only understand later in life.

Thank you, Tina, for creating "Broken Glowsticks." May your light shine brightly in all your endeavors this year.

Jessica Higdon

Contents

"Stars can't shine
without darkness."

– D.H. SIDEBOTTOM

From Loss to Resilience: A Journey of Healing and Transformation

— Amber Till —

As I stood there completely consumed with news, the air leaving my lungs, my legs too heavy to hold me up another second, I collapsed to the floor as my mother sobbed, "He's gone." Loved ones grabbed my arms to help raise me from the floor, but it was all too much.

It felt like my own life had ended.

I lost my right arm.

I went completely numb.

The hospital family waiting room suddenly felt different and cold.

Even with 30 people in there, it was all slow-motion and empty. It wasn't the same room I was in while praying to God just ten minutes ago, asking him to please let Aaron be okay and live through this.

It was now the room I wept for the loss of my big brother.

When I first heard Aaron had been shot, I immediately assumed the drugs and alcohol had finally taken over enough, and he ended his own life. Later, I learned this was far from the truth. Still, I had so much anger wash over me from the last few months of him battling his addictions, arguing with me over everything, even arguing at our last Christmas together two months prior -

I punched a concrete wall. I busted my knuckle open before even heading to the hospital.

I learned the news from a friend my mom had called and asked to break it to me because she was rushing to get to Aaron before it was too late. Sadly, my mom didn't make it to him in time and passed the ambulance on the way, praying it wasn't Aaron, but it was.

My friend was nice enough to drive me to the hospital and wait with all of us for the next 10+ hours. I could not take being in the waiting room with everyone crying while my brother was in surgery, so most of the time, I sat out in the hallway with my head buried in my knees.

The doctors did everything they could to save him, but the shotgun wound in his side was just too much on his body.

After his surgery, we got to take turns, two at a time, to go back and tell him goodbye. I was in denial and never said goodbye because I wanted him to wake up. I just wanted it to all be a horrible nightmare.

It still, to this day, feels unreal.

None of the situations were fair. I needed more time with my brother. I needed him to get the mental help he needed, to get healthy, and be happy in life. It was hard losing him for many months and knowing it "wasn't him; it was the addictions."

And then to have him be shot because of those addictions is now a part of my story that I get to live on to tell others.

That snowy, cold day in Mid-Missouri on February 27, 2013, completely turned my world upside down. You never think this stuff would happen to you, only in movies, until it does happen. My entire life could be one of those movies, unfortunately.

My brother and I were close in age and had the closest relationship out of all my siblings. He was my everything; I looked up to him for advice and wanted to be just like him for such a long time.

Until he lost himself a couple of years before his death made it official.

Aaron and I were both, sadly, abused, sexually and physically, as young children by a close family member. Our mother tried her hardest to get us all the help we could get, but it just wasn't enough at such young ages.

She would/will never give up on us and is incredibly strong for what she has gone through.

My mom never told me specifics, but I knew Aaron was abused worse than I was, and he had a few more years of it than I did. It makes me sick to my stomach to even talk about this 30 years later. I won't go into much detail about my abuse either, but I did know something wasn't right about the situation, and I told my family about the person at the young age of 7 years old.

That one evening, a very scared little girl asking questions to my mom changed the entire trajectory of our lives.

It took me years not to blame myself for the hard years that followed. Aaron and I did everything together; we were inseparable, even both testifying to send our abuser to jail. At this point, I was a 9-year-old terrified girl crying uncontrollably on the witness stand because I just wanted my mom.

Aaron was around age 13, and I can only imagine his emotions as a new teen. We weren't allowed to listen to each other's stories, and we honestly weren't allowed to talk about it to anyone except our therapists.

"That is not what you do," I was told multiple times while growing up.

But I know in my heart that my story needs to be talked about because the abusers in this world deserve to know how much pain they put on their victims. And victims need to know that their abusers had the power once but do not need control over your emotions anymore.

My brother and I had many very strong episodes of anger throughout our teenage years. We were the farthest thing from a perfect family unless you were on the outside looking in.

The therapist we had initially talked to did not do much to help us, and I honestly think they messed with our minds even more, but that story is for another day. And that is absolutely not our mom's fault, either; she didn't know any better and couldn't afford the best help.

I also started developing horrible chronic health conditions at such a young age, and I believe it is because my mind and body went through so much turmoil that my health took its toll because of it. I began passing out and often became very sick around 9 years old, the summer after my third-grade school year. Every day, I must deal with those health conditions and live with the fact that I never got a fair chance from the beginning.

I have been in the darkest of places multiple times in my life. The shame you wrongly accumulate from being abused, along with negative things you tell yourself, being bullied in school, being constantly sick, and so many other things, honestly stole so many years from my life, but I never gave up.

I watched others turn to drugs and destroy their lives, losing everything they owned. I told myself that I would probably like the drugs too much for my escape and would end up the same way, so I never once tried them.

I did turn to drinking for a couple of years, and it was a good feeling at the moment, but my health conditions worsened, and I paid the price for weeks on end from having just one drink.

Aaron, on the other hand, did not have the health issues I do, or maybe he didn't care about them enough. I know he began drinking and experimenting with drugs at a younger age. At first, it was to be included with his friends, but then it became a major problem.

You must understand how much I loved my brother, and I only talk badly about him to express the pain he must have felt to turn to the life he chose. I use his story to help others and know he couldn't be any more proud watching over me.

He only had a few short years of happiness in his small lifetime, which kills me the most. Aaron finally moved away, hit the top in his business, and was engaged to a beautiful soul, ultimately living his best life.

We had many fun times together during these years without any arguing. We could open up more about the things we both went through as children, which was nice to connect. But then he truly lost himself inside of the bottle again.

One night, after moving back home to my parents, he came home so messed up that he blacked out, peed his pants, and fell down the stairs.

He had officially hit rock bottom... or so I thought.

I think this was the night we (my mom, stepdad, and I) all realized Aaron had to get some mental help, or it would destroy us all.

We took turns driving him to his therapy appointments and ensuring he was taking his medications correctly, but he still struggled. It had to be his decision to change; no one else can take that responsibility.

It took me many years to accept that I had little control to help him.

During this time, we also had some big things happening inside our family's circle, and many changes occurred. I am unsure if that triggered Aaron because it greatly affected us. He showed up to Christmas 2012, messed up on who knows what, and we argued because he was being mean to me in front of everyone. I left in tears; that was the last time we spoke in person.

I tried to ignore him and continue with my life, thinking he would eventually snap out of it and get away from the horrible people he was running around.

Some of my friends couldn't understand how much love and hate I could have for him. But he was my brother, and we experienced our lives together. We went through way more than most people and did it together. To watch him literally drown and suffer was heart-wrenching and frustrating.

Six days later, on December 31, 2012, I was out celebrating New Year's Eve, having fun with friends, when I got a very weird text from Aaron, and I didn't believe what he was saying. That was the last time we ever spoke to each other, besides now when I see him only in my dreams.

Then, just sixty days later, he was gone forever.

The last week of February and the first week of March will now always be so hard for me and my family. Aaron was killed one week before what would have been his 29th birthday, March 5, 2013.

That year, we let 29 balloons go in his honor.

I had to help my mom let go of her balloon that read, "Happy birthday," as she grasped it tightly while sobbing again.

Everyone wanted this nightmare to be over... "it just couldn't be real."

I started seeing my therapist a lot more regularly, but nothing was helping me enough, and at one point, I stayed awake for an entire week. I couldn't shut my eyes, or I would relive everything all over again.

I decided to do what was best for me and help my family know I was safe, and I checked myself into a mental hospital. The doctors and nurses were all extremely nice and helped me sleep comfortably. I did some paintings and ultimately relaxed enough to leave just three days later.

That experience was the best thing I ever could have done for myself. I knew I did not feel safe to be alone, and my family had a lot going on while dealing with their own trauma. They would have cared for me, but I knew I needed more.

When Aaron and I were both 20 years old (4 years apart), we got a tattoo of a Bishop Chess piece to go with our family name. I, of course, had to copy him just like I did so many things throughout the earlier years. Later that same month, on March 22, 2013, my 25th birthday, I added to my tattoo with a balloon and Aaron's initials.

I feel like that is the perfect memorial for him.

It took us about six months to figure out his headstone and ashes. We laid his ashes to rest on September 7, 2013. I wept in that cemetery more than I had in a while; I could not stand the thought of leaving him there; I honestly thought about camping by his headstone.

The entire experience was a process I had to go through, and I had to take each day one at a time. I finally found comfort in knowing he was at eternal peace, with no more demons in his head.

Exactly two weeks later, on September 21, 2013, my world completely changed again, but this time for the better. That night, I met the man I would marry and live my dream life with.

Trevor has been my rock through many good and bad times, too. He has shown me what true love means for the first time in my life outside of my family. And he has taught me how to love myself as well, for the very first time.

When I am having a rough time with memories and flashbacks, he is always there.

When I am having a bad health day, he is always there.

I am so incredibly thankful that he came into my life, and the timing is not a coincidence.

On September 7, 2016, exactly three years after we laid my brother to rest, Trevor and I welcomed our baby girl into this world.

I cannot make up the divine path of my life.

Since then, we have also welcomed our miracle baby boy after losing two other babies. Our little family has grown in more ways than one, physically, emotionally, and mentally, and I am so proud of myself for taking each step forward to get to where I am today.

It would not be possible without my support system and everything I have ever been through to show me I am capable. This year, 2023, marks ten years, an entire decade since my brother passed away. I don't know how that is possible, but life does not stop, and we must live each day grateful and to the fullest.

About Amber Till

Amber is an internationally certified anxiety relief healer and master practitioner with a deep commitment to continuous learning and growth. Through her own journey of overcoming challenges, she has developed a passion for supporting others in their pursuit of mental well-being. As a wife and stay-at-home mom to two amazing children, she understands the importance of balancing personal and family life while prioritizing self-care.

Learn more at www.linktr.ee/atill22.

"She was broken, but never defeated. A diamond with a thousand cracks, still shining bright."

– UNKNOWN

The Broken Become the Bold

— Christina Whiteley —

The day I hit rock bottom, I was standing in my mom's backyard, back in my small hometown, and I just started sobbing. "Mom... I'm not okay. I'm NOT okay. And I don't know how to fix it." As tears streamed down my face, it was hard to pinpoint exactly what brought me to that moment; all I knew was that I needed help.

As someone who had been doing personal development for over 20 years and has her counselors and mentors on speed dial, I was shocked to find myself in this position. Was I not stronger than this? I have been helping entrepreneurs create their dream lifestyle while they earn their way to financial freedom, and here I was, unable to even get words out to advocate for myself.

The only thing that shocked me more than this moment was finding out that at 34, I had lived almost 20 years of my life with PTSD, something I previously thought only army vets and first responders had to face, and in this process, I had learned that it was my responsibility to fix it.

Except in that moment, I didn't know how. I was broken.

That August back in 2021 did me in. We had just celebrated my brother-in-law's wedding, which had been delayed for two years because of covid. My sister was about to have her second baby, and I was numb. I had just had my second miscarriage. The first one was earlier that year. It was even more devastating because after I had called my sister to tell her I was pregnant, we discovered that we were both pregnant and due within 3 days of each other that coming August.

This loss not only triggered postpartum depression (which I then experienced AGAIN after the second miscarriage), but it put my sister and me in this weird place where she felt unnecessary guilt for her healthy pregnancy and I gathered all my strength to be happy for her, while grieving my own loss.

This coincided with covid lockdowns, which meant we were also in isolation, social distancing, masking, and made to stay home, which, turns out, isn't good for anyone's mental health. This kept us from family support during this really difficult time, but it also kept me from medical care.

I went through both miscarriages, without in-person appointments, at home, alone, with no post-care from a doctor. I requested a specialist appointment, as now I was convinced that I was incapable of conceiving, but that maybe I was slowly dying from something on the inside. I was told it would be a four-month wait for a phone appointment, and only then would she deem it necessary to book an in-person appointment if needed.

During this time, I was skeptical of the covid vaccine because of its quick release. I know, don't bring it up, right? Don't question the science! I get it. But as I was trying to have another baby, I did have some concerns. Being in the health and wellness space for the last seven years, having to advocate for my own health for years in the medical system, and knowing we are not legally allowed to recommend ANY natural supplements to pregnant or breastfeeding women, I was just a little apprehensive knowing that this vaccine had been given emergency use permission and that doctors were unable to give me any long-term or even a full list of side effects. I was considered high risk after two miscarriages and in my late thirties. I wasn't going to do or try anything that could take away from a chance that we could conceive again.

And before you call me an anti-vaxxer... I've had all my vaccines since childhood and many more to travel the world... I never questioned the efficacy of a vaccine or the side effects until now. People I loved asked me if I was "really" skeptical or just being difficult. They would email me articles showing recommendations for pregnant women and how dangerous COVID-19 could be if they caught it without being vaccinated. But my gut feeling kept pushing back because I needed more solid information, and it simply couldn't be provided to me at the time.

Then it got weird. If you didn't go along with it, you no longer had the same privileges as people who did. We became second class citizens overnight. My grandma asked if she would ever see me again, and it was only then I realized the depth of fear that people had towards those that did not vaccinate - even in perfect health.

We noticed our family didn't get invitations to group functions (not that we could have gone to these outings, of course, because we didn't have a valid vaccine passport at the time). We noticed people starting to avoid us or conversations with us for whatever the reasons may be.

Clearly, the fearmongering through media, which bled into our society, had affected how people viewed us, and even with optimal health, chose not to spend time with our family. Our circle grew smaller, and my husband and I realized that maybe the support we thought we had wasn't the community we had at all.

In September, our daughter, on her request, started French immersion in kindergarten. She is a happy, outgoing kid who makes friends easily. She's the kind of kid who engages the shy kids and includes them with the group. We were so proud of her, and then started to notice, she was worrying more about little things.

She was struggling to learn a new language with masks and distancing. Then, a couple of times, she came home, disturbed, asking questions that were out of character. It was clear to me that the conversations she was having at school in her class were not age appropriate.

She started feeling unsafe at school and it took me two weeks to convince her she was safe there. By the beginning of October, I told my husband, Ryan, "I don't want her there anymore. These precious young years of her life are the most impressionable. We can do a better job of being a role model for her, then the school system at this point." Parenting was a commitment I wasn't willing to compromise on, and we knew then this was the right move for our family.

A couple of days later there was an announcement on the news that they would be closing the Canadian borders to those who had not received the COVID-19 vaccine, meaning we would no longer be able to leave the country or fly within the country if we didn't go against our intuition and comply with what was requested.

My core value of freedom was being tested daily, and I was in fight or flight, constantly living in the vibration of being under attack. My husband looked at me that night and said, let's go to Mexico. Let's take the free work trip you earned, that we initially decided against, and stay for a few months - just take a break from this all and get a balcony view of our lives and how we want to live out our next chapter.

That was my "START THE CAR" Ikea moment when I simply said, "YES! Let's do it!" Never in a million years did I think he would agree to live abroad away from my family to embrace this adventure with our family, but secretly, I had been dreaming about it since I was a little girl.

Little did I know that my husband recognized that I was not okay after the past year, and he made the suggestion to save me. Ladies, find yourself a man who knows what you need, before you have to ask for it, and that love will continue to grow for decades.

In two and a half weeks, we packed up our 3,200 sq foot home and left all the boxes in the basement. We cleared the closets and staged the house, as we thought if we decided to stay longer than a few months, we could rent out our home on Airbnb and pay our tenants living in the carriage house or a rental company a percentage to manage it.

When our plane landed in Cabo, and the warm air hit my skin, it felt like we were in a parallel universe. Like we had stepped out of one world into another. It wasn't just the weather – that was to be expected going from gray, wet, cold to the warm, sunny desert – it was the energy. It was different here. I didn't feel this oppressive cloud over my head, and I felt like I could finally relax into vacation mode, which we hadn't done in a couple of years because of the pandemic. We turned off all Canadian and US media and started to embrace the sunshine and our new chapter here.

We immediately met people who supported us in our decision to bring our young family to Mexico, and they praised our bravery. These people from all over the world became our community and supported us and our daughter in ways I am forever grateful for. We created closer relationships with friends in Cabo San Lucas within a few months than with our neighbors back in Canada for the past ten years. Ironically enough, we felt so much safer here.

It was in January 2023 that we decided to burn the boats. In the fourteen years we've been together, my husband has only come to me twice and said, Christina, we either sell the house now or sell in 10 years when the market returns. My husband has been creating wealth in real estate, flipping properties, and timing the markets with his real estate knowledge since he was 19. He's really good at it.

So, I said, now… like RIGHT now?

Or do we have a few months to decide?

NOW.

He said we must decide now because the market will turn in the spring. So, we took our emotions out of it and made a profitable decision. We sold the house within a couple of weeks.

Now we had really committed to this Mexico adventure, so we had to start getting our lives in order down here and creating a schedule for our daughter around her education.

Two years in now, she is almost bilingual and has made many friends, many who don't speak any English. She is outgoing, curious and adventurous. If I've learned anything, it's that travel is the best form of diversity and inclusion education you could ask for.

We also experienced what it is like to become an immigrant. I have a lot more empathy for others that have been through this process. It is no small feat, but it is doable if you have a desire to relocate.

Some pretty incredible things have happened since we decided to make the leap and take advantage of a terrible situation and turn it into our dream life. We learned that with courage, you are rewarded, and that risk is equal to the size of the reward.

My husband and I became closer in this move because we realized so many of our actions had been previously decided with the benefit of everyone else in mind; and in the process, we had forgotten how to put each other and what we truly desire first. We knew that if we stayed in Canada, we were being set up to lose, even with a high income, and for what we wanted to do in life, we had to make some sacrifices to get ahead.

I started talking about our move online. I had been in network and affiliate marketing for seven years after closing down my salon and had been teaching people how to build a business around their lifestyle, but now here we were, actually doing that on a global scale.

My videos had millions of views, and people started reaching out. The UK Mirror did an incredible article titled, "Couple work from the beach and live mortgage-free after quitting city life." It wasn't until I started getting random messages from people online that I even knew how big that publication was.

Next, I had the owners of the Mexico News Daily reach out and ask me to write a 6-part series on our move from Canada to Cabo San Lucas as a lifestyle piece. We have since continued that partnership because this is the biggest English-speaking publication in Mexico, and 80% of the million subscribers live outside of Mexico and want to move here. We give them our unique viewpoint and share our experience in the hopes that if the reader is looking for adventure but just a bit apprehensive about the move, we inspire them to start living life on their own terms, too.

My following has grown exponentially to over 170,000 now across all platforms. Although it may not be the biggest following you've seen, I've got a community full of people who are freedom motivated and willing to do what's hard to live this way, too.

Then, Miss Tina Torres called me and said, "I have a special project I want you to be a part of with me and two more of my friends." That's when the Uncensored Entrepreneur was born, and we started doing weekly talk shows with a combined audience of almost one million people.

I would never have had the exposure or street cred necessary to expand my business and help people the way I do now if we had not dared to leave what was comfortable for adventure, but that decision alone gave us purpose and saved our mental health.

It's not enough anymore to post pretty photos and highlight reels on social media because people have a healthy skepticism of what's real these days. You must live your beliefs and values and have conviction in whatever you choose to do to help people. Technology and AI will turn the world upside down, but I also believe it's a tool we can use to grow, learn, and develop ideas into assets faster.

Now more than ever, we need to lean into our gifts, master them, and use our unique life experiences to help those through the things that almost killed us.

That is true leadership.

Being able to express vulnerability and empathy, with respect and understanding, while helping people overcome the challenges they currently face with gratitude and grace.

Taking the opportunity to learn through these challenges, and instead of letting them beat you up, let them guide you. Let them bump you in the right direction when you're not paying attention or are making decisions that are not for your greatest good. The lessons keep showing up in your lifetime until you choose to learn from them and move forward. That's next-level growth right there.

Without the pressures of COVID-19, the miscarriages, and our core value of freedom being threatened, we never would have made this move. I am so grateful for these things now, and I see these obstacles for what they were: a stress test to prove our strength. With every negative thing that happens, you can either learn from it, grow from it, or avoid it the next time. Without adversity, we don't gain our strength.

It's those that are broken who become the brave and the bold. They are the ones who inspire through what they have overcome, not what they have achieved.

About Christina Whiteley

Christina is a born entrepreneur and a strong advocate of creating your dream lifestyle while creating financial freedom. Her influence extends beyond her teaching platform as she shares valuable business building ideas and inspiration on podcasts, speaking engagements, and through social media. Her ultimate goal is to empower others to create multiple streams of income, and to pursue their dreams and live a fulfilling life that they are inspired to build, while being a great role model for their kids.

For several years, Christina successfully owned and operated a salon and onsite wedding business, where she enjoyed working with her clients. However, she felt a deep desire to make a bigger impact and empower others more profoundly. When her daughter was born, she embarked on a journey to become an expert in business strategy, online marketing, and leadership, so they could not only thrive in business, but with their family as well.

Learn more about her at www.christinawhiteley.com.

"Sometimes it takes a broken heart to come back even stronger."

– UNKNOWN

From Broken to Bald to Brilliant

— Christine Rodriguez —

I was broken long before I hit my breaking point.

My mother abandoned me when I was three years old… and again a few years later after she came back into my life.

I was molested by my uncle for several years, starting when I was 4 or 5 years old.

I started masturbating regularly at 12 years old.

I lost my virginity at 15…just to do it.

I started losing my hair at 16 years old.

I was raped at 17 after getting blackout drunk for the first time… the month after I graduated high school… by an airman I had just met that same day through a mutual friend.

I was raped a couple of years later after joining the military by a so-called male friend and fellow airman… drunk in my own dorm room.

I became extremely promiscuous.

I had no self-worth.

I had low self-esteem.

I had suicidal ideations.

I battled depression and anxiety.

I went head-to-head with infertility for five years.

I conformed to those around me and the world I lived in… I rarely had original thoughts or did anything authentically for myself.

I was just a puppet on strings… doing what everyone else wanted or expected me to do… and I rarely spoke up or challenged them otherwise.

Despite all this, I married my amazing, supportive husband in 2006. I had three phenomenal children; my first, born in 2011 at 28 weeks' gestation via classical C-section, weighed 1 pound, 14 ounces - by definition, she was a micro-preemie.

I became a very successful and decorated military veteran, serving 20 years before retiring in 2014. I enjoyed assignments in Florida (literally stationed in my hometown), Germany, Guam, and Arizona. I spent time in Cameroon, Africa, and the island of Dominica performing dentistry as part of humanitarian efforts.

Through unconventional paths, I found my way to homeschool, be an entrepreneur, and to do things on my own terms, even if it meant going against societal norms and standards and despite what other people thought of me because...

"What other people think of me is none of my business."

- Wayne Dyer

How did I find my way?

I hit my breaking point in October 2020, a week after my 45th birthday.

You hear about mid-life crises all the time. Was this MINE?

See, I was standing in the kitchen with my husband, sobbing. He was drying the dishes and putting them away. I had walked in with determination. If our kitchen had a door, I would've flung it open, and it would have looked and sounded like I stormed in. I was focused on sharing what I was about to unpack on him.

I began, "I feel like I'm meant for more. There's got to be more to life. I know I have a bigger purpose. I don't know what that is. But I need to find it. I need to figure it out."

My husband listened as he always does when I bring him my crazy, ambitious ideas or antics.

Just to let you know, I'm a creative. And I'm a problem solver. So, I'm continuously developing new, visionary ways to do things. I'm constantly going from one project to another. Or I'm inventing multiple ways to do the same project in different ways. And this was all the same.

Some may say I'm fickle. I first heard of this word and learned its definition in high school when I was given this label, especially after having a new boyfriend every two weeks (or so it seemed). Although fickle might be appropriate in some contexts, I think identifying as a creative is much more suitable for who I truly am.

Now, at this point in my life, I had already been a part of an amazing network marketing company for four years. I had recently joined two other companies within the past two months, too. Little did I know, I was actually searching for more meaning in my life.

At this moment in the kitchen, when I was expressing myself to my husband, I realized I had come to that proverbial fork in the road and that the road I was on had been traveled via cruise control while asleep at the wheel. Or I had just been the passenger in my own vehicle of life, allowing others to drive it for me.

I had no clue how I got there. I had just been going through the motions.

For those who lived it, you know 2020 was the year of the pandemic = COVID-19… Coronavirus. And it changed many lives in many ways globally.

My husband, the kids, and I had traveled to Phoenix, Arizona, in February 2020 for Spring Training as we attempt to do every year. The pandemic in this timeline was in its infancy and was very unfamiliar. It was a week after returning home that the world went into lockdown.

I would love to use the pandemic and the lockdown as an excuse for influencing me to indulge in extreme spending habits, but that existed long before COVID-19. See, I've been struggling financially since I was 18 when I joined the military in 1994 - bounced checks, credit card debt, title loans, debt consolidation, etc. I even pawned my possessions to get some cash or to pay a bill.

I have always made financial decisions based on instant gratification.

I want what I want when I want it.

And in 2020, still, nothing had changed.

Completely behind my husband's back, I had already started to acquire new credit cards at the beginning of the year. I discovered virtual credit cards. And if I could opt into a payment plan, I was all for it. "Buy now, pay later" was a hook, line, and sinker for me.

I was oblivious, but I was on the road to rock bottom.

It became an addiction. As long as I got approved, I kept applying for more credit.

Before I knew it, I was over $35,000 in secret personal debt... my husband had no clue!

I was buying stuff for the house, stuff for the kids, and stuff for the office. Stuff. Stuff. Stuff. And more stuff. None of which I needed, most of which I kept hidden from the hubs.

I was investing in an insane amount of personal and professional development courses.

By the time summer came, I was focused on my mindset. I was diving into books and programs that would help me shift my mindset to a more positive lifestyle.

If I thought it would help me and change my life, I was consuming it. By the time my 45th birthday came in October, I was chock-full of information. I had been massively consuming ideas, knowledge, and courses but doing absolutely nothing with it.

I had acquired so much crap, too. Things. So many materialistic things. Just more things to clutter the countertops, tabletops, and corners of our home, only to collect more dust.

It would be like buying a brand-new car and just letting it sit in the garage, never using it for what value it provided.

Shit.

With $35K, I could've bought a brand-new car!

Mind blown.

We all learn lessons in life. This was a very, very, VERY expensive one.

Perspective.

But like I said before, I was searching for purpose and meaning, and maybe it was even a cry for help - I just hadn't realized it yet.

Until that day in the kitchen, when I was sobbing to my husband, I knew I had a bigger purpose and needed to figure out what that was for me.

My entrepreneurial heart began constructing business concepts, ideas, and ways I could utilize the triple network marketing companies I was now a part of to further my life's purpose.

What was my life's purpose?

I knew I wanted to serve, maybe even teach, but that was about it. I would learn later that I needed a "why" and that the "how" would work itself out.

I spent the next few weeks contemplating this, that, and the other. I had no definitive answers. I had no clarity.

At the beginning of November 2020, as part of the many professional development courses I had invested in that year, I joined a 14-day live challenge - going live online every day for two weeks. Within that would be homework and tasks to help grow me and my business.

Challenge accepted.

It was on like Donkey Kong!

Except on the third day, I was ready to quit, give up, throw in the towel.

Typical.

Yep, that sounds like me—all my damn life, starting something but never finishing it.

On day 4 of the challenge, I woke up, and first thing that morning, I watched a replay of a live from a woman in a Facebook group that I'm a part of - it was a hair loss support group.

On her live, she had shaved her head. She shared her story and her reasons for doing it.

I saw her courage, her determination, her vulnerability, and I felt her strength, her liberation, her POWER.

And in that moment, I knew exactly what I needed to do.

I must shave my head, too.

See, I started noticing my hair thinning when I was 16. My parents took me to a dermatologist who ordered blood work and found no cause for the hair loss.

I was thankful to have been healthy but also frustrated not to have definitive answers.

My hair loss progressed.

I wore baseball hats often. And although I rocked hats with style, it's not something a woman wants to accessorize with when wearing cute outfits. Baseball hats do not go with everything.

I rarely wore a wig but did so on occasion. For me, the thing about wigs was that I always felt uncomfortable, almost fake and phony.

I went through a phase where I dyed my hair black.

I used powdered hair-building fibers. Great concept. Very messy.

I wore my hair pulled up all the time. Serving in the military made it easy and "normal" to do. But when not in uniform, I did it, too. I had one hairstyle all the time. Up.

Ten years later, while serving active duty in Guam, I noticed quite often that when conversing with friends and co-workers, I could follow their eyes, their gaze, up to the top of my head; they were looking at my baldness, not my eyes - there was definitely no eye contact.

I developed a complex. I became even more conscious of my thinning hair, so much so that it affected my duties.

So, I saw a military dermatologist who took biopsies from my scalp.

Again, the results returned - no known cause for the hair loss.

Medical mystery.

Or just female pattern hair loss.

…okay, so back to the day four live.

On November 7, 2020, I publicly shared the reasons for shaving my head.

Here is a summary from that live:

Have you ever wanted to do something but were so stuck in your head that you couldn't move forward?

When we get stuck in our head, our mind becomes the obstacle.

The hair on my head serves no purpose for me. And although I'm rocking the hats and wigs, I'm hiding behind them, behind the hair loss.

When you hide behind something, you're not being your true self, and for me, it creates a lot of anxiety and prevents me from doing things I really want to do. I hold back.

Pushing outside my comfort zone challenges me to go to the next level.

When we have fear, we often don't talk about it... and don't work through it... we hide. And that can be a big barrier to achieving what we want in life.

I want to walk out, be free, and be my true self - to feel comfortable!

I know by shaving my head, I can be my true self because once I do this, I can't hide anymore.

Society says that women should have beautiful hair, and you grow up getting that stuck in your head that women are supposed to look a certain way and they're not supposed to have short hair, or a buzz cut.

People can be cruel, but I don't even care what people think, anymore. I create my own happiness.

I can only control my thoughts, my feelings, and my actions.

I cannot control what other people do, and even though that can take a toll on you, people can be mean and stare. When people do those things, you are challenged to be stronger than that. TEACH YOUR MIND TO BE STRONGER THAN YOUR EMOTIONS.

Shaving my head is symbolic to me - like a butterfly coming out of the cocoon.

I'm gonna create my own happiness. I'm gonna do this for me.

Maybe I will inspire you to do something BOLD, and something BIG, and something BEAUTIFUL for yourself.

You gotta do it scared! If you live your life scared, you'll never grow, you'll never get there, you'll never get to your dreams, you'll never do it big, you will never because you're just gonna be scared.

So do it scared… and then, when you see that you survived or it's not as bad as you thought, then you can do anything.

You can watch the entire live video here: https://www.facebook.com/christinerodriguezonline/videos/10217384493660404.

So, yep! I shaved my head.

With my husband's unconditional support, he shaved my head for me. You can watch that video here: https://youtu.be/m0xcoQTjSis.

So, I did it, y'all!

Yay, me!

I would love to share with you that although I was scared and nervous to take such an extreme, unconventional approach to solve my hair loss problem, I do not regret it.

Imagine my hair loss as an armored cloak. It was shielding me from doing things with my friends and family. I would say "no" to doing most things even though I wanted to, so in essence, I was not living my best life.

Doing this literally shed that armor… it liberated, empowered, and set me free.

And it inspired me to do more.

Now, I'm on a mission to help other women look, feel, and be their best selves.

I might've been broken long before this breaking point, but I wholeheartedly believe that it's not what happens to you; it's what you do with it that matters most.

Be you. Do you. For you.

About Christine Rodriguez

 Christine Rodriguez is a retired U.S. Air Force veteran of 20 years, a stay-at-home, homeschooling, entrepreneurial wife, and mommy of three, a self-proclaimed "expert" problem solver, a creative, an author, and everyday teacher, coach, and mentor.

She is on a mission to guide, inspire, and empower her two young daughters and her only son… along with other amazing women… to look, feel, and be their best. She wants to encourage everyone to accept themselves for who they are, to unconditionally love themselves first before loving others (because you can't give what you don't already possess), and to keep a positive and open mindset while attracting a happy and fulfilling lifestyle.

"Stars are born from chaos. The most beautiful souls emerge from the deepest of scars."

– UNKNOWN

Take the Steps and Know You Are Worth It

— Cora Mae Spalding —

Sitting on the living room floor of my gorgeous new apartment, I couldn't decide if I should go work out or drink myself to death, two polar opposites, but both were my only choices in December of 2019.

It was gross outside in Minnesota, gray and cold, like my soon-to-be ex-husband's heart. Just after the 5th Christmas with my now husband, I had moved out of our house the day after we spent Christmas together. Everything was falling apart; everything I had worked so hard for was crumbling in real-time.

I thought about his face when I told him I had gotten an apartment and how he smiled and looked relieved and happy, which was (again) the polar opposite of what I was hoping for.

He talked about just "taking a break" and "seeing if I could stay sober," which made me feel like I was some kind of disposable person to him, not the person I said "I do" with and made a promise to God that through thick and thin, we would be together.

What a fucking liar.

So, on my floor in my overpriced apartment, I sat in this weird state of mind as I felt my heart break into unfixable pieces. I was contemplating suicide for the first time in my life... and I had a lot of struggles in my life.

You name it, I experienced it. Bullied as a kid, my father was an alcoholic; my parents fought so loud I would hide upstairs consoling my brother, who was five years younger, and cried when they got really loud.

My dad died when I was 14 because he was loaded and crashed his jeep, killing him, and as people always have to say for some reason, "at least he just killed himself and no one else."

I had a couple of good boyfriends in my life early on. But then I seemed to steer toward real narcissistic douchebags that liked to treat me like some dumb whore; beating me and raping me, cheating on me, and then crying wolf when I would try and leave.

So, I started to drink heavier and heavier. Oh yeah, I forgot to tell you that I started drinking when I was 14, on the night of my father's funeral, and didn't stop until I went to treatment at 35.

I knew I had a problem, but I also had this crazy woman inside of me who kept saying, "You can sober up on your own; you have before, just don't go back again."

And I would for months at a time!

When I met my husband at 31 years old in 2014, I was not drinking (or trying hard not to drink), and we hit it off

SO GOOD! Our first date started with lunch and went late into the night - and sober!

I never wanted it to end, and as I told him, I don't kiss on the first date (because I was actively trying not to date anyone seriously after escaping a VERY abusive man just six months earlier). Still, he went in for a kiss, which felt so good.

Life was good with him for a while, he asked me to move in, and I did. I tried so hard not to get "too drunk" around him, but that happened eventually, and it just kept happening. He was nine months sober when we met, and as I fell deeper and deeper into my addiction to alcohol, he grew further and further away from me.

What's interesting looking back is that my husband had a lot of mental and emotional issues he had not worked through and was struggling with while, at the same time, I was struggling not to drink.

There were months I would be sober, and he was just the shell of a man. He would go into these very dark moods, and it felt like I didn't even know him.

It felt as if his soul would leave his body, and he would hide in the basement of our home. And I felt like a total nobody to him even though we slept in the same bed every night.

Months went by without sex or intimacy, and I knew that my husband wasn't exactly the romantic type (ok, not at all!!), but it was just soul-crushing that the man I loved so deeply didn't seem to love me back anymore.

I'm the kind of woman who loves romantic bullshit, adventure and someone who loves me hard! I crave flirting, banter, kissing, foreplay, and that stuff those bad boys used to provide me. But there I was, married and miserable.

Now, I haven't told you yet that I am gifted with many "Clair" abilities, and you probably have heard the word "empath," so I can use that to describe what I feel with other humans and their energies.

My whole life, I have experienced the ability to feel other people's emotions, feelings, and energies. Many times, people have asked me, "How could you know that about me?" or "I haven't been able to put into words what you are describing that I am feeling or have felt in the past."

Still, the downside to this is I can't help but feel when those closest to me are suffering, lying, hurting, in denial, and all the "bad" stuff, too, and my husband was a major trigger for me and my self-soothing.

I never had a word for these abilities until this year. I was finally able to look into this, and now I fully embrace these abilities because they help me to be a phenomenal coach and healer. I turned all these "unfortunate things" I was made of into a source of power to become a badass woman who helps other women step into their own power.

So how did I get from someone struggling between working out and drinking herself to death on that cold, gross day, sitting on the floor, oozing out misery and ready to die to what I am today? I am so glad that you asked!

That day, I decided not to work out; I chose a 1.75 of Captain Morgan rum instead. I hadn't bought booze in over seven months. This harsh guilt suffocated me as I got the bottle home, got a glass, and had my soda pop ready.

My hands were shaking while my mouth was drooling, thinking about that first shot entering my mouth and going down my throat and that familiar warm sensation that goes through my whole body when the body realizes, "Oh hey, we just consumed a large shot of booze!"

I got drunk as shit, and I didn't stop for over two weeks. Every day, I drank deeper and deeper into my grave. My husband came over a few times because I refused to see him, and he knew I was spiraling down. I remember that he called one day and said a really nice treatment center had space for me and asked if I was ready to go, and holy fuck, was I ever!

He took me there, and many things happened while I was there for the good and bad. I got to "dry out" and was forced to deal with my broken heart.

See, the husband was still hell-bent on divorcing me, and I was pretty sure he was also seeing another woman from his work (damn that intuition!)

So, I cried a lot and one night, I was woken up from sleep, and the full moon was bright as can be and huge in the sky. I love the moon, and it was like she woke me up and called out to me, "Cora, come to the window, get on your knees, and start praying," and that is exactly what I did.

I begged God to help me keep my husband and my life. I begged God to keep me sober for the rest of my life, and while sobbing uncontrollably, I promised myself that I would do whatever it took to get my shit together and stay that way.

Shortly after this, I was notified that I had to leave treatment at just three weeks and couldn't stay for my 4th week. I was bummed because I wanted the help, but I knew God was getting me home to start becoming who and what I was born to be!

My husband refused to come to get me, so I had to wait all day for a ride from the treatment place, and that 3-hour drive home in the back of that van was one of the longest rides of my life.

I was excited to get home but scared to death as well. I lost my job the day I went to treatment, and I was so scared because I didn't have any money, but all I wanted to do was go home to my husband and our home and my fur babies.

That night, my grade school best friend came over and spent the night with me; I could feel that something was very wrong with what my husband had told me about why I couldn't get some things from the house, so at 9 pm, my friend and I drive to the house, and he wasn't there.

He was with that woman I had assumed he was with, and he left there to come to talk with me. We spent over 45 minutes talking in this ice-cold drizzle, and I could tell he felt like a piece of shit for being over there. I asked him to attend church in the morning, and he said, "We will see." That next morning, he declined.

I knew it was over then, and for some reason, I went to church ready to say goodbye to him in my heart or at least begin the process.

While walking in, I saw his car and was shocked and shaken. We sat by each other during service. I held back tears while I sang my praises, and at the end of service, he turned to me and said, "Can I come over? I really need to come over and talk to you," and he looked really bothered and was forceful...

I got home expecting him to bring the divorce papers, so I let him in, tried to be tough, and stuck my hand out for some papers. But instead of papers, he started sobbing and grabbed me in the tightest hug I had ever had in my life, and although I could barely understand him, he told me that he loved me more than anything and wanted me to come home.

My whole body started to tremble! I couldn't believe what was happening, and I immediately went back to that night on my knees, talking to God and the moon, and felt this feeling of pure love and joy and knew it was God saying, "Here you go, Cora, here is your life back."

This was January of 2019, and I moved back home the next month; God found me a renter, and I could not have been more in love with my opportunity never to look back and start my fucking life!!!

Since then, many amazing things have happened; we even sold our house and moved south for a new life and warmer weather!

I got a job right away, and then a new job once we moved and created a six-figure income by 2020 working for a Fortune 100 company.

We continue to work on our dreams, and as of January 2022, I left the corporate world after I refused to get vaccinated, and I also refused ever to have a boss again!

I worked on opening my coaching program, investing around $25,000 in myself to be one of the best in my field.

I now help women launch their own high-ticket coaching or healing business online and organically, living my absolute best life, fulfilled and badass.

There are many more details to my story that I haven't included, but my point is that no matter what you have experienced and how badly you have been broken, you can heal.

And once you begin the healing journey, you begin to see how big and bright your future can be! Instead of being on a downward spiral, you are on an upward spiral to better and better!

I am very spiritual, and much of my journey has included leaning on my intuition and tapping into my authentic self. My best advice is to start ignoring all the noise around you and listen to your gut.

We all have this Divine connection to God and the Universe, and we will never be steered wrong when we trust the process and take control of our emotions and outcomes in life.

One of the most fulfilling parts of my coaching program is the fact I get to help these women rise up while they are building their business, and when it gets hard or feels like it's "too much," I can offer them clarity, peace of mind, and hold space while they work through it all.

The most common fear I hear is fear of failure, and the second is feeling not good enough (or not knowing enough) to start their own coaching/healing business.

This is where I get to share my own personal "failures" with them and give them space to feel all the emotions that come up and not hide them or feel shame for them. I let them go through the experience and teach them to be accountable for their actions and emotions! It's a blessing to watch women crack open that shell they have been hiding in and step into their True Potential and Divine Feminine!

Every woman has choices, and only they can make them. Even if you have had terrible things occur in your life, you can choose to take the smallest steps at first to change the trajectory of your future.

Imagine walking in a straight line - what happens if you turn your right foot just 15 degrees to the right and start walking? Your results and destinations are drastically different from that original path, aren't they?

That is how I did it, day by day and even hour by hour. Almost five years ago, I was trying to kill myself, and now I'm sipping cucumber water, sitting at my desk in my brand-new loft, in my robe, and in a custom-built home we just finished building. Please take my advice, take the steps, and know you are worth it.

About Cora Mae Spalding

Cora Mae Spalding is a phenomenal feminine sales coach who empowers women to unlock their full potential by teaching them the foundations of organic sales strategies for their online businesses.

With a deep passion for freedom and independence, Cora believes in breaking free from limiting beliefs and societal expectations to create a life of fulfillment and purpose.

Cora faced numerous challenges growing up and was often told she would never amount to much. However, these obstacles only fueled her determination to prove the naysayers wrong. During this transformative journey, Cora discovered her true calling and embarked on a path to help others do the same.

In 2022, after experiencing the disappointment of being fired from a six-figure sales job, Cora turned adversity into opportunity. She seized the moment and launched her own successful business, driven by a desire for time and financial freedom. Through her coaching and healing services, Cora aims to inspire other women to break free from the corporate grind and design a life that aligns with their values, allowing more time for family, travel, and pursuing passions on their own terms.

Not only does Cora bring a wealth of personal experience and resilience to their coaching practice, but she is super fun to work with, and all her clients agree that she is a foundational pillar in their success with their online business!

With her unique blend of expertise, compassion, and unwavering commitment to empowering women, Cora Mae Spalding is available to work with individuals ready to embark on their own transformative journey toward creating a life of purpose, abundance, and personal freedom.

Learn more at www.facebook.com/groups/wildwealthywomanclub.

"In the darkest nights, the brightest stars are born."

– UNKNOWN

The Not-So-Magical Place in Life

— Janet Favela —

They say time heals all. I say that is such bullshit.

Time passes without our consent, and we just heal ourselves for the sake of survival.

They also say that in life, we will have life-defining moments that will change the course of our lives. At the same time, I have had enough in my time to last the rest of my life, but when I close my eyes and think of one in particular.

I think back to a day in 2017. It was spring break, yet nothing about it was of blossoming Spring; rather, it was about the break, the biggest break of my life, the breakup of my lifetime.

I had just landed in Orlando, FL, with my two little girls, and they were excited and exhausted from the flight and long day. They anxiously awaited this moment as Disney World was their childhood dream destination.

Standing in a long, hot line to pick up my rental car, I was relieved to see I was next in line. I was on a time crunch since my phone battery was low, and I had no apps or information on my phone for the time being. I didn't even have any photos on the device.

The previous night had been one of the worst nights of my life, and my husband had deleted everything through my iCloud.

As I walked over to the man behind the desk and handed him my driver's license and reservation number, I could see the light at the end of the tunnel. It was getting dark outside for my girls, who I could tell were getting super sleepy. After waiting in line for over two hours, a shower and bed seemed like a sweet deal.

"Your card is declined; next person in line!" yelled the man. I wasn't upset or worried, knowing I had money in the bank account, so I calmly asked if he could swipe it again.

He seemed upset and again shook his head. "Lady, nope," he said as he insisted I return to the back of the line. I just couldn't bear to put my girls back in that line, so I stalled.

I grabbed my phone and couldn't check my balance on the app, so I started calling and texting my husband like a lunatic—no answer, twenty more calls later, and nothing.

"Get out of the line, "the man shouted, "no," I said as I stood there frozen. I started thinking about the bank not allowing the transaction because I was traveling, so I called my bank immediately.

I felt my heart pounding heavily, and my face was on fire. I was starting to panic a little; I thought about how I had failed to prepare correctly with everything going on the night before.

As I remained on hold, all I could think about was that this was the worst timing to find out about my husband's affair the previous night. How would I focus or enjoy this precious time with my children?

When the representative finally got with me, he explained how the account was closed off, and I wasn't on that account any longer, "What, how?" I yelled. Hours earlier, I had been, this made no sense.

It then hit me at that moment that this was no mistake and that I was no longer his wife in his world. The room was spinning and blurred out like in a scene of a drama movie. I began to think how that could be; he wasn't that kind of man, and we were both account holders and although he was more of the breadwinner, I also contributed to the family and worked hard.

I had just closed two clients the week prior and deposited one check the previous night with the other in my bag to deposit. That was the first time I had a complete panic attack and an overboard anxiety attack.

Worse, I had no idea what I was feeling or what it was. I was thirty-two and somehow had made it through life that long without those feelings before; I was frightened.

I wanted to scream and cry so loud that God could hear me in the sky, yet I stared into my little girl's innocent eyes and knew I had to get my shit together.

I started to slow my breathing; I knew I couldn't scare my girls or worry them at all; I wouldn't ruin their moment... after all, this was supposed to be the happiest place on earth.

I looked for an outlet to charge my phone, but I only saw one in the middle of a cement post in the middle of a drive-up lane; I thought this must have been a bus stop turned into a car rental location.

I had my little girls sit on a bench with all our belongings as I walked backward, staring at them with the fear of wandering too far from them; it was terrible. However, I had to connect my phone to turn it on.

I attempted to call their father repeatedly, but he never responded or called me back the whole night. I tried to give up after 30 calls, yet I kept going with no luck. With no phone contact, I downloaded my Facebook app, desperately attempting to seek help.

I was able to message a friend in Florida who I knew from being an Army Spouse. She didn't respond right away because we didn't speak regularly. I held both of my daughter's hands and kissed them with hugs so tight it looked like I was doing it for them, and I was, yet I needed them so much at that moment. I assured the girls we would soon be at a hotel.

I couldn't even get an Uber without the app or card attached to my account; I didn't even know where I would get a penny from at that moment.

It was the scariest moment of my life. I had credit cards but hadn't prepared much otherwise with the drama unfolding. How could I have been so dumb and senseless, I thought?

I wasn't afraid for myself. Being an only child with a single mother working two jobs, being without a father my whole life, and being bullied for being Mexican American in grade school had set me up to be tough and independent with survivor skills while being left alone.

This was much worse as I had the most important job to protect and provide for my babies; it was a good thing we had left my two-year-old son with my mother after discovering I would be taking the kids to Disney alone.

I had to protect the two precious pieces of me at that moment. As my girls started dozing off on my lap, I quietly started hyperventilating,

"Stay calm, Janet," I told myself, "You have been through worse situations in life and made it out alive. Think like a grown woman, and remember, you got this."

I then remembered my next-door neighbor, an agent like myself, was always on her phone and would answer and could go next door to get my husband's attention and tell him it was an emergency.

Her number was on her business page, so I found it, and when we would text or snap, she would instantly reply. After twenty attempts, nothing. I was moving on to my next solution when she finally answered," Thank God, "I said.

I asked her for the favor, and she responded that she wasn't home but would have her niece go over and notify him. That notification never came.

I then called my in-laws after remembering their number; they were completely concerned and did their best to help me, yet they were not tech-savvy enough to send money or help immediately.

They hurried to my house and, upon arrival, called me to inform me he was not home. My heart sank completely, for I knew at that moment what was would never be again.

From that day forward, I knew my life would never be the same again. My best friend, my high school sweetheart, my husband whom I had shared my entire adult life with, the one I had started a life and family with, the one I always felt safe around, protected by, loved by, was gone.

We had been together since the summer I was sixteen, and we had just celebrated our thirteenth anniversary that last November as well as renewed our marriage vows three years prior with a beautiful wedding and my white dress, the wedding I had waited ten years after the marriage union in a courtroom to have.

It was all over forever; he didn't love or care about me anymore. Until that moment, I felt I could fix everything, even the infidelity from the previous night. No one was perfect, and who was I to judge?

However, not loving me anymore, that was unfixable. If only God would hold truth to the scripture, "What God joins together, let no man tear apart."

He was always such a good-hearted man, provider, and protector. Sure, he wasn't affectionate; however, who would be after two tours in Iraq? I always thought that he would do anything for his wife and children.

I no longer knew the man; he was no longer there.

About Janet Favela

Janet Favela is a mother of three who resides in Texas and is a real estate agent. Better known in her area as the Pink Realtor, she does everything pink and wears pink daily, making her branding extra unique.

She has been a multi-million-dollar producer for the last few years; she is also part of the Malouff International Group at Keller Williams Heritage and has over 15 years of experience.

In her field of work, she started real estate in Lawton, OK, where she is now a leader in her marketplace and always gives back to her community in any way she can.

Her passions include making memories with her children and traveling every chance she gets (to tropical places when possible). She desires to leave a legacy for her children someday through real estate investing. She also enjoys working out, reading, cooking, baking, and anything crafty.

She is a Top 100 Latino agent in The National Association of Hispanic Real Estate Professionals. She is on the Agent Leadership Council in her office and holds many chairs and positions across multiple boards.

Learn more at www.kwsanantonio.com/our-agents/janet-favela-ramirez.

"From the ashes, we rise.
From the pain, we grow.
From the darkness, we
become stars."

– UNKNOWN

From Ashes to Embers

— Jill Albanys —

The darkest storms seem to roll in as the light of day is lost in the soul shadowed by night. This is the moment when joyful expectations become elusive, and the visionary's sight is blotted out by gray. After years of being 'faith-full' and highly motivated for great things, I found myself sitting under the shade of fear.

The spirit of heaviness as a garment weighted in lead seemed to bind me tightly in despair as I wondered if life was even worth living. My once bright future became a gloomy forecast as hope deferred and left my dreams to die in the wake of the relentless storm.

How did I end up here? A girl, once fearless and brave, was now broken and full of anxiety concerning her future and what it would bring. It was a crying shame… and I did, thousands and thousands of tears…

As I look back to the beginning of this journey, back to childhood, I remember the daily struggles of our large and impoverished family. The simplicities of running water in the bathroom, indoor toilets, or a thermometer placed on a hall wall to ensure warmth were all luxuries we did not have.

One of my earliest memories is of my mother placing a washtub tin on the floor and filling it with hot water that came freshly heated by our kitchen's old wood cook stove.

The warm water would serve to bathe one child and then be used again for the next. I remember the matted gray tub seeming huge to me as a child.

Now, I see it was quite small, and the youngest of the children were most blessed to sit in the steamy pool. The older children would take sponge baths in a basin filled with a gallon or two of water.

Though we were poor and had limited resources as children, I grew to have the ability to see beyond what I could see. My mother had a big part in creating a world bigger than the one we lived in. Through her love of art, music, and faith in God, she painted pictures of a life that 'could be.' It was a life I wanted.

So, I began to dream, and dream big, concerning music. I was sure God had great things for me. My mother could go before me to open one stage after another from when I was very young. I obediently stood before hundreds of people, which seemingly defied all odds. I felt destined for the platform. I loved to sing.

As I grew older, I met a good man, and we married at a young age. Though we were happily married, financial struggles continued to haunt us.

Nevertheless, he became my rock, offering unwavering support as I embarked on my journey towards a music career. I persisted, living with the mindset that anything was possible and challenging myself to expand my wings of faith.

After a few years of recording and writing songs, I traveled to Nashville, Tennessee, singing on stage and appearing on unpopular TV shows. I would hear my mother's voice echoing in my head, recounting the story of Loretta Lynn. My mother believed if Loretta could overcome poverty and become a successful singer, so could I, which was quite inspiring for a small-town girl such as myself.

With this wind beneath my wings, I knocked on one door after the next. I went from the United Artist Tower to Music Row, meeting countless individuals in the music industry and playing my humble demo CDs for them. Eventually, I landed a three-year contract with a producer in Nashville. It felt like my dreams were finally coming true. "If you can dream it... You can be it!"

But then came the shift. It was a bright, sunny afternoon, and it seemed time had frozen, granting me a precious moment to reflect on my life. I had just returned home after visiting my producer and touring the studios.

I glanced around at our modest early 1900s home filled with my young children's laughter and joy, and I realized the true and profound price of success. At that moment, I reevaluated what truly held value in life, leading me to decide to step away from my long-sought-after career in country music.

What mattered most to me was right in front of me. I was already successful. My heart was to create a faith-filled environment for my children to grow in, and instead of singing country music, I knew I was called to utilize my gifts and talents to advance the Kingdom of God.

Walking away from the enticing contract was a bold move, but I took the leap of faith and have never looked back. Within a short time, I was invited to become a worship leader in a small country church my family attended.

For a while, life seemed perfect. I was content to serve God in a humble capacity. My love for music intertwined seamlessly with my passion for people. My heart's deepest longing was to walk alongside others, guiding them toward a better, more fulfilling life as they grew in faith and embraced abundant joy.

However, as time passed, the walls of my blissful life began to crumble, and everything I thought was safe and secure started to fade away. I was being called to a higher ministry level, and with it, the battleground intensified.

Embracing the mantle of preaching the gospel, it seemed like the forces of darkness unleashed their fury upon me. They say, "The higher the level, the bigger the devil." And I found that to be true.

I share this story to emphasize the state of being devoid of dreams that I found myself in. I went from Music Row to a pile of ashes. During my descent into the valley of despair, one verse became ingrained in my mind: "Where there is no vision, the people perish."

Never did I imagine that I would become someone without a vision, yet alas, I did. I found myself blind and groping for something to believe in.

Nothing quite compares to the suffocating hopelessness that extinguishes a once-burning ember, making us wonder if it will ever ignite again.

One may question what caused me to plummet so low. I can attribute my descent to a few arrows that pierced my heart and inflicted great soul-deep sorrow. A wise saying goes something like this: "If you live seeking people's approval, you will perish under their criticism."

As I embarked on my journey as a minister of the gospel through music and the spoken Word, I became a target for opinions and slander. This experience was almost unbearable for me as someone with a compassionate heart and driven to serve others.

But, my friend, when all hope seems lost, a rising sun breaks through, ushering in a new morning, leaving yesterday's trials to fade into distant memories.

The valley has passed. The battle has been won.

One of the most significant outcomes of this arduous battle was my newfound resilience against people's opinions. My war nearly ended in defeat as I contemplated abandoning my calling, but instead, I chose to stand and keep speaking hope to others.

My journey now inspires women everywhere, encouraging them to fearlessly pursue their dreams, fulfill their divine callings, and rise above the judgments of others.

Today, I assist other women in living free and prosperous lives as they step into their calling and grow their coaching and consulting businesses. Where once I inspired just a handful of people, I now impact hundreds of women by telling my story.

Friend, I encourage you to persevere and press through your challenges. Your broken places will become the very things that allow your light to shine the brightest.

So go ahead, my sister. Stand for your calling, and your dream, and never let anything dull your shine!

About Jill Albanys

Having experienced both poverty and abundance, Jill's personal journey from a challenging background has ignited her fervor to guide women towards financial freedom. She is committed to supporting them in pursuing their God-given purpose while spending time doing more of the things they enjoy with the people they love.

When you embark on a journey with Jill, you're not just investing in your financial future—you're embarking on a transformative experience that will awaken your spirit, amplify your influence, and empower you to live a life of abundance and purpose. Join Jill today and discover the extraordinary possibilities that await you.

Learn more at www.elmlink.co/kingdominfluencers.

"She had been through hell, but you wouldn't know it. She still had a fire in her eyes and a spirit that refused to break."

– UNKNOWN

Your Inner Fire: Igniting the Journey from Unworthy to Unstoppable

— Dr. Kimberly Olsen —

"Motherhood is the exquisite inconvenience of being another person's everything."

~ Unknown

Have you ever found yourself mindlessly scrolling through Facebook or Instagram, only to stumble upon a picture-perfect woman with her gorgeous children, living in a stunningly gorgeous home, decorated top to bottom with farm chic decor? Did you feel a pang of envy or inadequacy? Did a slew of not-so-great feelings wash over you, driving you to seek solace in the carefully curated world of Pinterest? If this is the new standard in the age of social media, we may find ourselves in deep trouble.

If we are expected to smell good, have flawless makeup, sport freshly washed hair (sans dry shampoo), and never wear the same yoga pants two days in a row, then I can confidently say that I will never make the cut for this unattainable model of perfection.

No way.

There have been days when I barely found the time to shower or brush my teeth, let alone accomplish anything else on my never-ending to-do list.

If this is the relentless benchmark against which you and I are measured, it's no wonder we often feel like failures. We are constantly bombarded with the notion that we are not good enough. But that's not how it's supposed to be.

We are meant to feel empowered, strong, confident, and unstoppable. We should revel in the glory of keeping our children alive for another day, raising our hands to high-five our spouses once the little ones are snugly tucked in for the night.

We are meant to feel like total badasses.

Yet, as I work with countless women every day, I see that this is far from the reality for many of them. Am I right?

But deep down, I know you want to feel that way. I can sense the desire burning within your heart. And that's precisely why you picked up this book. To tackle all the challenges, gain a firm grip on life… find the elusive balance in your own life that you know is attainable.

I'd love to share my personal journey of how I have been able to shine my own light bright like a glowstick. I'll give you a little spoiler alert – it was definitely a dull and fading light at one point. If you can resonate with that, let the words on these pages give you hope that you, too, can ignite your own inner light.

Hot Mess Express

It was a scorching fall day in 2016, and I found myself trapped in gridlocked traffic in my sweltering black Highlander. I was pumping. No, not pumping gas or something more glamorous, but rather full-on breast pumping—an experience that any mother knows is far from enjoyable.

After enduring a grueling ten-hour workday, followed by over two hours of commuting, all I could think about was getting home and opening a bottle of wine. The well-being of my 2.5-year-old daughter, Addison, and my nine-month-old baby, Elise, didn't even cross my mind. Dinner plans were a distant afterthought.

Instead, my thoughts were fixated on alcohol.

Now, I'm aware that many mothers in my circle would often joke, asking if it was "wine o'clock" yet. In fact, I would frequently find one of my former neighbors sipping wine in the front yard when I returned from work. It wasn't an uncommon sight.

However, the difference with my longing for a drink that day was that I felt a genuine need for it. In Rachel Hollis's book, "Girl, Wash Your Face," she shared a powerful chapter about her own struggles with alcohol.

She emphasized the distinction between wanting a drink and needing one.

Alcohol had become my coping mechanism. The previous year had been a whirlwind. We discovered that we were pregnant with Elise on Addison's first birthday, and I was already in my second trimester by then.

By the way, how does one not notice a tiny human growing inside them for 14 weeks? That's a question that still baffles me. I guess it really demonstrates how detached I was from my circumstances.

Six weeks before Elise's arrival, I lost my fancy corporate job and bid farewell to my salary and maternity leave benefits. It was a devastating blow, and fear gripped me like never before. How were we going to welcome a new baby while struggling to pay the mortgage and daycare expenses? The weight of financial obligations loomed large.

If you're living paycheck to paycheck, you understand the mounting pressure of unexpected expenses. Imagine your air conditioning system breaking down and being forced to cough up $3,000 in cash. Could you handle it, or would you have to resort to your credit card? I understand the dilemma all too well.

Shortly after Elise's birth, I managed to secure a local job after five months of unemployment. I had been hustling non-stop since she was born, even running a boot camp in my backyard with her strapped in a baby carrier to my chest. This new job opportunity was on the other side of town, but it was better than facing another month without employment. And so, the cycle began.

Overwhelmed with two little ones in diapers and lacking confidence as a new mother, I was drowning in a sea of anxiety. My job was dreadful, and one of the managers seemed to relish bullying me whenever he had the chance.

Resentment and frustration simmered within me, fueled by the fact that I was missing out on my girls' precious milestones. I barely spent an hour with them each day during the week. I yearned for a way to be present and available for them.

Ironically, despite my background in fitness and nutrition, I had zero time for exercise and felt perpetually stressed out. I looked at myself in the mirror and hardly recognized the person staring back. How could someone with my knowledge and expertise feel so disconnected from her own body? Have you ever experienced that?

Fast forward to the summer of 2017, when I stumbled upon network marketing. Initially, I experienced some success, but I needed more time to focus on my business amidst my job and the demands of raising a young family. I went from my first commission check being over a thousand dollars down to $200 a few months later. I felt sick to my stomach.

I knew deep within the depths of my soul that I was self-sabotaging… yet again. Here, I had this amazing opportunity to get my family out of debt and turn our lives around, and I was throwing it down the drain. I decided enough was enough, and I enlisted professional support to overcome my decade-long battle with alcohol abuse finally.

It took a lot of work, but after six weeks, I finally stepped into celibacy and have been celebrating ever since😊. This is when I was able to start seeing myself as worthy, good, valuable… God had put me on this planet for a reason, and I was going to figure out what that was!

One particular day, I found myself sitting at my desk, tears streaming down my face. I had just dropped off Elise at preschool despite her running a temperature of 100.1 degrees. My husband, Scott, couldn't take time off work, and if I stayed home, I would lose out on all my commissions. Every penny counted, and we needed every single one of them. At that moment, I silently prayed to God, desperately seeking a way to grow my business without sacrificing my already hectic life.

That's when I discovered some incredible trainers in the network marketing industry who taught the art of building businesses on social media.

No in-home meetings? Check.

No evening events? Check.

No extensive traveling to launch teams and leaving my family behind? Check again.

It sounded like a perfect fit for me. I could actually do this!

I started going live weekly on Facebook, sharing the knowledge I was acquiring with my growing audience. Week after week, I went from no views to a few, and then, gradually, I began to gain traction. The flood of messages pouring into my Messenger inbox was overwhelming, and I struggled to keep up with the daily influx of DMs. My first Facebook group soon followed and rapidly grew into the thousands.

Women messaged me, expressing their appreciation for my genuine and authentic approach. Most of them had grown weary of the spammy tactics employed by many in the network marketing industry. They longed for a mentor who could guide them with honesty, integrity, and practical strategies. That's when it hit me—I had a responsibility to help these women find their way.

But how could I mentor others if my own life was in shambles? I couldn't continue down the path of exhaustion and burnout. It was time to take control, reclaim my life, and rediscover balance.

The Awakening

The alarm clock screeched at 5:00 a.m., and I groggily rose from my bed. The day was about to begin, and I had a choice to make. Would I continue with my old routine of rushing through the day, barely keeping my head above water, or would I embrace a new approach?

That morning marked the beginning of my awakening—a shift in mindset and a commitment to finding balance. I made a promise to myself to prioritize self-care and create a life that honored my values.

Over the next few months, I embarked on a journey of self-discovery and personal growth. I devoured books on mindfulness, productivity, and time management. I attended seminars and workshops, seeking wisdom from experts who had mastered the art of balancing motherhood and success.

But it wasn't just about acquiring knowledge; it was about implementing the strategies and principles I learned. I experimented with various techniques and crafted a routine that worked for me—a routine that allowed me to be a present and engaged mother while pursuing my goals.

I learned the importance of setting boundaries and saying no. I discovered the power of delegation and asking for help when needed. I found joy in simplifying my life and focusing on what truly mattered. And most importantly, I realized that self-care wasn't selfish—it was essential for my well-being and the well-being of my family.

Through trial and error, I honed my time management skills and developed strategies to maximize productivity. I created systems and routines that streamlined my daily tasks, freeing up precious time for activities that brought me joy and fulfillment.

As I transformed my own life, I began to share my journey with other women. Through my podcast, social media platforms, and speaking engagements, I encouraged mothers to embrace self-care, pursue their passions, and create a life they love. I witnessed firsthand the impact my words and actions had on these women, and it fueled my desire to help even more.

And so, with that being said, I now empower you on your journey to balance and fulfillment. Plug into a community where you can be supported as you navigate the challenges of entrepreneurship, rediscover your passions, and create a life that aligns with your values.

Are you ready? It's time to embark on this transformative journey and step into the highest version of yourself!

About Dr. Kimberly Olsen

Dr. Kimberly Olson is a self-made multimillionaire and the creator of Goal Digger Girl Co., where she serves female entrepreneurs by teaching them simple systems and online strategies in sales and marketing.

Most recently, she received the honor of being chosen as the 'Top Business Innovative of the Year' by the International Association of Top Professionals. Kimberly has been featured on the cover of Success Pitchers Magazine as a 'Self Made Social Media Mogul,' as well as 'Top 10 Most Ambitious Women in Business to Follow.' She is a TEDx speaker, and her recent speech was listed as one of the '10 Top TEDx Talks that You Don't Want to Miss.'

Kimberly is also the founder of the non-profit Elephant Sisters and has two PhDs in Natural Health and Holistic

Nutrition. She is the author of seven books, including several #1 international best-sellers, has a top 25 rated podcast in marketing with over 700,000 downloads, and has reached the top half percent globally in network marketing. She has recently shared the stage with Rachel Hollis, Erin King, Keri Ford, and Jessica Higdon.

Learn more at www.thegoaldiggergirl.com.

"She turned her wounds into wisdom and wore her scars like stardust."

– ATTICUS

Surrendering Your Shame

— Linda Ann Barber —

Imagine the fear and struggle of trying to get out of a burning building in the middle of the night.

After making your way out, you go back in the morning to observe the destruction.

You see the landscape charred. The roof collapsed.

The windows are blown out. Your belongings are lost.

The devastation cripples you with wonders of how you will rebuild from here.

This is the crippling feeling I felt standing at the foot of my bed in 2017. I stood in the ashes. Our home was in foreclosure; my car was repossessed; I was without electricity and sleeping with a flashlight; my food source was elevated to a local food bank; my bank account was shut down.

Despite three years of throwing water on it in an effort to save it, my world felt as if it was burnt to the ground.

Shame was ruling my life. I had a war going on in my mind greater than any judgment I felt around me.

I was ashamed of the men relentlessly banging on my garage door to take away my Lexus.

I was ashamed of sleeping with a flashlight.

I was ashamed I couldn't give my son more for his college needs.

I was ashamed I was looking for change in my car to buy food.

Simply, I was ashamed I failed.

Failed? Well, it's what I felt so strongly at the time.

I'm not sure that anyone knew the extent of my pain and struggle. I hid a lot, yet I'm not sure how well.

A good friend and I would walk most nights. I recall asking her to walk early without telling her I wanted to get home to bed before it got too dark in the house. Fearing more judgment, I didn't want to risk the neighbors seeing me using a flashlight in the house.

There did come a point when I had to humble myself and ask for some financial support. It allowed me to put out small fires temporarily, but the coals were hot, and the fire was relentless. Being unable to rebound and pay them back in the time I had hoped, more shame and frustration piled on.

In a state of shame, our brain thinks there's danger, which causes us to fight, flight, or freeze. I was always a fighter, but this time was different. I was losing my grip. I began to freeze.

I was tired. I felt as if a concrete wall was built in front of me. I personified this tiredness as 'weakness,' which, as you can imagine, only fueled the shame.

No amount of self-worth could shine through until I surrendered it. Unfortunately, shame seemed to be the only thing I had a grip on!

To my surprise, a day came that was different from these last three years.

An overwhelming feeling came over me as I stood at the edge of my bed on that hot summer day. Not caring who would hear me, I screamed out loud:

'I freaking deserve better than this!!!'

I had a twinge of recalling who I was.

The woman who protected and provided.

The woman who was recognized professionally.

The woman who was resilient and built a life for her and her son.

The woman who bought and improved homes single-handedly.

The woman who cared for others.

The woman who got this far in life despite great adversities!

It was enough to hold me while 'I stood back up' for a moment. I was done crying.

I was done worrying.

I was done giving power to my fears.

I was done wondering what others were thinking of me.

More so, I was done shaming!

I was ready to surrender my shame!

In this surrender, I grabbed my journal from the nightstand, sat on the right side of my bed, and began writing.

I wrote about my life. No. Not my past. No. Not my current circumstance. I wrote about the life I would start living once I put my pen down!

In detail, I wrote about my career, including how I would lead a team while earning over six figures. I wrote about our new 'home.' I even described the furnishings: white furniture and white carpet! I know, crazy, right?

I wrote about the places I shopped, the meals I hosted, and the fun I was experiencing with my son, family, and friends. Over four journal pages, I detailed my life around relationships, money, faith, fitness, and well-being.

Now, mind you, if you were looking over my shoulder as I sat there writing, you would say, 'This is all positive and nice, but let's just get you some groceries!' Looking back, I laugh because it seemed like the logical thing to do.

But I had a different plan.

In my surrender, I was committed to reframing my life!

For the first time in my life, I focused solely on ME and what I wanted and deserved!

In search of love, approval, acceptance, etc., much of my life, I looked at what I could do for others. I was the queen of people-pleasing and proving myself worthy.

Yet, sitting on the bed, I loved myself enough to ask, 'What do YOU need?' 'What do YOU want?'

I chose ME!

So, you may be wondering where this fiery destruction began. Let me bring you back three years earlier to 2014.

My son went off to college. As sad as I felt with the ending of football nights, Wednesday game nights with 'BreakDin' (breakfast for dinner) for dinner, music blaring from the garage, basketballs bouncing in the driveway, laughing with parents on the bleachers, etc., I also felt excited for this being MY time! Time to focus on myself!

I was excited about meeting friends for a martini or having cereal for dinner.

No schedules. No homework. No sports. No demands. Just me and our 12-year-old lab, Nick.

I was just a couple of months into this new empty nest phase when things began to break down. I had resigned from a 22-year financial advising career with the dream of building in the world of entrepreneurship.

And to fill an income gap and a health insurance need, I took a temporary job at an auto & home insurance agency.

Outside of roaming in circles around the house while I adjusted to the quietness, life was pretty good.

One night, I came home from a night out with girlfriends. Everything was normal. I was feeling happy (then again, I did enjoy some wine!)

Yet, I felt myself come out of my body when I fell asleep. I thought I was dying. Literally! Scared, I jumped to my feet and turned on the light.

After settling down, I dismissed this episode by thinking I was overtired (or the wine was kicking in). I turned off the light and went back to sleep.

But a few nights later, it happened again.

I connected these episodes to my new job. Since my advising work offered flexibility and a sense of freedom and the new job did not, I thought it was the culprit for the change in my health.

Thinking that feeling restricted was triggering my anxiety, I thought looking for different work was best. Feeling confident in my abilities and with a couple of months of savings in my account, I resigned.

Unfortunately, I soon found out the restrictive job was NOT the culprit.

These out-of-body experiences came more frequently.

I was growing more scared of dying alone.

Anxiety began filling up my day. I was pushing through but confused as to what was happening.

Weeks of this went by, and then the scariest of days happened. I felt a gun at the back right side of my head.

'I'm going crazy!' I thought.

Despite fearing my doctor would also think I was going crazy and possibly institutionalize me, I was fully transparent with her about these nightly experiences and the gun sensation against my head.

She referred me to a psychiatrist who didn't take long to diagnose me with PTSD.

Although, at the time, I thought PTSD only happened to our military men and women, I was somewhat relieved that there was a reason for all I was experiencing. Yet I couldn't understand WHY this was happening now!

I need to give you a glimpse of the previous 12 years to understand. My psychiatrist and I started my healing from the same glimpse in our counseling sessions.

Over these 12 years, I experienced moments of barely surviving to moments of thriving after leaving the marital home in 2000 with just my clothes and a few items for my son. I began to rebuild a life for us with just a clock radio as our starting point.

I still have this clock in my closet as a reminder of what's possible despite adversity.

I had fun experiences with my son and his friends, family get-togethers, getaways with my boyfriend, time with friends, etc., yet at the same time, I was also experiencing pretty stressful events.

So, I'll highlight just some of the events that supported the PTSD diagnosis:

- I was juggling a demanding financial career while, at times, being a full-time mom.

- I refused to surrender the court fight despite being warned by three court-appointed psychologists that my life was under threat and to seek protection.

- I did my best to create a fun, 'normal' home for my son, hoping he didn't notice I was sleeping outside his bedroom door or crawling across the floor in the middle of the night to check on him while my ex-husband hid outside.

- I watched my credit tumble and retirement accounts being depleted in order to meet attorney expenses of up to $14,000 per trial -- and we had many!

- After 5-6 years of exhausting 'family counseling' efforts, and the court encouraging a healthier father-son relationship based on feedback from several professionals, my back was against the wall. The pediatrician stepped in and referred my son to an intense evaluation due to the stress he was exposed to. At this same time, I visited with the psychiatrist. I decided to verbally express to the court my willingness to surrender the care of my son to the State in lieu of a doctor putting a pill in his mouth or him having to experience another day in the documented toxicity of supervised visits (damn, this makes tears rush down my face every time I remember this day).

- I was waking up most mornings thinking, 'What can I teach him today?' not knowing if it was my last.

- I walked out of court with a great deal of fear for my safety (years later, I learned that cops would follow me at a distance to make sure I was safe).

- I tried dating yet hid my fears and daily experiences in greater fear that he would break up with me and something good in my life would be lost.

During this time, I went out of my way to paint a picture that we were living a 'normal' life, so friends and family didn't worry about us. I often felt alone, yet it was my choice.

I don't share any of this for you to feel sorry for me. I certainly don't share to brag. I did what most parents would do to protect the best interest of their child.

I share these events to say, 'WHY now?'

I experienced a great deal of anxiety over the 12 years, but why didn't I have out-of-body experiences and fear to this extent back then? Back when I was IN the fire?

I was frustrated!

As I'm sure you can see, the answer was right before me.

My body did its job; it cooperated in a way that helped me to survive all those years, and now it was my time to heal.

The psychiatrist explained it was my subconscious (that was in survival mode) now having space to breathe. And in this space, it was making itself known!

Looking back, I believe God chose this healing period on purpose. My son was tucked away at college, which gave me more time to focus on myself.

In joking (but somewhat serious), I even questioned why God didn't wait until I had a few martini nights with friends under my belt or maybe some fresh air in my lungs after preparing for a graduation and a college move.

It taught me that healing times can be messy and confusing, but NOW is always best!

Now that you know where the fire started, let's return to my bedroom. That 'glowstick' moment at the edge of my bed where I decided I was worth shining bright again.

I finished writing out what my soul was asking for without judging it with wonders of 'How is this going to even happen?' Now, it was time for me to take my first step!

My first step was to line up with my desires and BE HER NOW!! Sure, it appeared I didn't have much to work with, especially no money. In these moments, it's much easier to see what we lack and quickly feel it's a hopeless endeavor. But I had something incredibly valuable to me on the inside.

I began a journey of aligning; aligning to the woman I wanted to become.

I no longer focused on my circumstances. Instead, I became best friends with my (inner) resources: my self-talk, boundaries, identity, and connections were the start.

Feeling better, I used what I had available to reclaim a little bit of peace and power each day!

You may be wondering where all this got me.

Within eight months, I sold my home in a short sale and felt good about paying off my mortgage debt with equity; I moved to Colorado to lead a team while earning over six figures. AND I lived in a luxury apartment with white furniture and white carpet!

I'm not here to say there haven't been challenging times over the last six years since this 'glowstick Moment,' but here's what I've learned from this experience and in helping my clients spark what's inside them:

You, too, can create the life experiences you desire when you activate what you have available inside you and NOT give your power to your circumstances!

I spent many days avoiding the mirror because I didn't like the woman looking back at me. The shame was too great. Since surrendering my shame, I allowed more of the woman I am on the inside to come out!

I'm proud of 'her' for living in HER truth and allowing herself to shine! And each day, I've learned to love her more and more!

My beautiful 'glowstick' sister, it's time.

It's time to surrender your shame and ignite what's waiting on the inside of YOU!

You, too, are worthy of shining bright and living your best second half of life!

About Linda Ann Barber

Linda is a bold force in sparking new meaning for living in the second half of life! With a proven track record for reinventing her life and business at 46 and again at 51, she has become a sought-after life coach for women 45 - 90+ years young!

As the CEO of Linda Ann Barber Coaching, LLC and creator of the Live Alive Blueprint™, Linda has helped countless women shift from feeling unmotivated, confused, and doubtful to embodying a whole new level of excitement, purpose, and aliveness in their second half!

After a 22-year Financial Advising career, Linda adventured through a new industry where she consulted renowned speakers and coaches. A few years later, she answered a higher calling that led her to empowering women through her own story!

During this time, she moved from her home state of NY to Colorado while transitioning from a somber empty nest to experiencing a fun, new 'adult' relationship with her son and a renewed friendship with herself! Today, she helps other empty nesters do the same!

Linda is the Podcast Host of The SECOND HALF LAB Where your Second Half is your Best Half. She is a blogger and contributing author and is currently writing her first book, which will be published in 2024.

Linda is the woman to help you spark aliveness in your life and business! Learn more at www.lindaannbarber.com.

"A broken heart is an opportunity for growth, a canvas for resilience, and a beacon for strength."

– UNKNOWN

The Power of Pain: A Story of Hope, Healing and Moving Past Infidelity

— Sal Harper —

Being a mom has always been a struggle for me. I didn't grow up wanting to get married or have a bunch of kids.

When an abnormal pap smear confirmed that I needed treatment for cancerous cells in my cervix, the result was that I might not be able to have children. And I was okay with that.

According to the doctors, even if I did get pregnant, I may not be able to carry the pregnancy to full term because of all the damage the treatment would cause.

So, years later, when my husband and I miraculously gave birth to our firstborn, we counted our blessings and immediately tried for a second just in case the fertility gods decided one child was enough.

My second pregnancy didn't go as smoothly as the first.

Right from the get-go, it was a complicated pregnancy. I was already considered high-risk because of my medical history and age.

I battled morning sickness every day well into my second trimester; at 20 weeks, I started to consistently have preterm labor contractions that put me on 100% bedrest at 31 weeks. By 32 weeks, all the medicine in the world didn't help with those contractions and couldn't get me to full-term because my little one decided to arrive two months early.

Again, we counted our blessings and thanked our lucky stars that we were now a healthy family of four.

Being a mom didn't come naturally to me. I struggled with motherhood immediately after giving birth. I had NO CLUE what I was doing or how I should raise a child, let alone two.

The day before you give birth, you THINK you're prepared. You nest, buy everything you imagine your baby will need, and then BAM!

Suddenly, you have this tiny little life in the palm of your hands that is totally dependent on you for everything.

Fear started to set in because I realized there was no way this baby could verbally communicate with me his need for food, sleep, or a diaper change except for the wailing of his cries and screams.

I haven't read a single book on the market that adequately prepared me for parenthood, regardless of what developmental stage my children were in, not as a newborn, an adolescent, or a teenager… especially not as a teenager.

I did what most people do; I hoped for the best, prepared for the worst, and prayed I wouldn't screw this up.

If you're a new mom like me, trying to juggle motherhood while keeping the house clean, the laundry folded, the dishes washed, the lawn mowed, the dogs fed, and the kids out of trouble, romantic time or any alone time with your husband can be scarce.

Especially when you're sleep-deprived and stressed out, while the slight smell of residual vomit still lingers in your hair, and you haven't showered in nearly a week… You aren't feeling your sexiest.

How could I, when I've been taking care of everything and everyone else in the household instead of the most important person in the world… Me.

Every so often, in those early hours of the morning, just before dawn when the kids are still down, my husband can pull me over to him, make love to me, and tell me he loves me, that suddenly, I can feel sexy, loved and desired again.

But on this day, it was a different day.

It was one of those early hour mornings, and we had just finished making love. I lay tightly snuggled in his warm, muscular arms, feeling safe and intimately connected to him.

I was planning my day and had a list of a dozen to-do's running through my head when suddenly, I felt a strange wave of calmness pass over my entire body... and I just knew.

Out of the blue, I had this thought. I can't explain it, and to this day, I still can't understand it.

Life was great! I was happy. I was on top of the world, and everything was as it should be.

I loved my life and cherished what we had spent all those years building together.

I was a proud wife and a stay-at-home mom, and I had two beautiful kids who were both miracle babies.

Everyone told me I was married to a hot husband who looked like Bradley Cooper.

We had a big house, drove luxury cars, and my husband made a six-figure income that could afford us the lifestyle we had always dreamed of living when we were young. Life was, if you will, picture perfect.

But on this day, it was different because I just knew.

It wasn't a feeling, and it wasn't a thought. It was an overwhelming sense of KNOWING... that my husband... was having an affair.

I began to sob quietly to myself, my body starting to shake. My husband suddenly awoke and quickly sat up, asking me what was wrong.

I could tell by the look on his face that he was very concerned, almost horrified, because in all the years we had been together, he had never seen me cry... not once.

"Babe, what's wrong?" he asked again, in a sterner voice.

A minute passed and then another. The silence was in the air, and I could feel everything I had worked so hard to build slowly slip away in those early dawn hours.

I broke the silence with a hard sniff. Wiping tears from my face, I gently said... "You're having an affair, aren't you?"

He lowered his head, pierced his lips, and began to cry, then softly whispered... "Yes."

Whether your discovery was a text on his phone, a secret Tinder account, the faint smell of perfume on his shirt, or an unusual charge on your credit card statement... I will never forget the pain and anguish that immediately engulfed me when I heard that single word... Yes.

The next ten years were a complete haze and a blur. I drifted by in life, just trying to survive. I spent the next ten years clawing my way out of the crater-sized hole this bomb just left after tearing apart my life, family, and marriage in the blink of an eye.

Emotional triggers, intrusive thoughts, and negative self-talk haunted me around every corner. I couldn't eat or sleep, and each day, I floated through the motions like a poorly programmed robot.

We spent years in and out of therapy, attended couples' workshops, communicated more, started going to church, took more trips together as a family, went on date nights every Thursday, and even had more sex.

But like an earthquake that leaves a permanent gaping crack in the foundation of your home, nothing is ever the same... not a single holiday, not a single birthday, and anniversaries only served as a reminder that our marriage was vulnerable and had been infiltrated by another woman.

Trust is broken, dreams are lost, and my only thought is... Will I forgive or ever be able to trust my husband again?!

It took some time to find our rhythm, but it felt like things were getting back to normal. I was smiling again, I became more social both in and out of church, and we started building a new life together.

And then it happened again.

Out of the left field, BAM, he tells me he's leaving me… for another woman… a much younger woman!!!

ARE YOU FUCKING KIDDING ME?!?!

After all this time and all the money we have spent salvaging our marriage and putting the pieces of our relationship back together, you tell me NOW that you haven't been happy for a long time and will be much happier with this other woman?!

Was it me?!

Was it something I said?!

Was it something I did?!

What about the kids?!

What about me?!

What about the last twenty-one years together?! Did it mean anything to you?! Was it all a lie?!

"I still love you," I said, "despite everything you've put this family through."

"I love you too, but I'm just not in love with you anymore," he replied so coldly, so callously.

I could feel the knot and vomit rising from the pit of my stomach, my knees giving in as I dropped to the ground. My face became flushed, and tears started streaming down my face uncontrollably.

I couldn't wrap my head around what he was saying. I couldn't understand why he was doing this when I did everything right.

What was I going to do?! He moved me three thousand miles away from my home, friends, and family. I felt so alone.

I didn't have a job or money, and I wasn't sure what I was supposed to do next.

I couldn't think, I couldn't see straight, and I couldn't catch my breath. All I could do was gasp for air and curl into a ball as my heart pounded.

Over the next few months, he really did move out. He really did leave me for another woman… a much younger woman. And the grass really did seem greener on the other side.

Regardless of the circumstances, I had to figure it out for myself and the kids.

I did what I could to make ends meet and provide for me and my boys. I sold things around the house; I got a job, and as a friend said, I pulled up my big girl panties.

But the next fourteen months were excruciating!

I couldn't stop crying, I couldn't stop calling him, and I couldn't stop begging him to come home.

I couldn't sleep, I couldn't eat, and I couldn't stop drinking to numb the pain. There were so many days that I couldn't get out of bed and even take care of the kids.

I lost my job, I lost fifty pounds, and I had lost my husband. Nothing seemed to matter without him being part of the family. I thought my life was over, and I didn't think I could do it without him, so I decided to end it all.

I tied up loose ends, closed accounts, gave things away, and made arrangements in my will for my mom to take care of my boys.

That day, I sent my kids off to school and sat on the couch, taking everything in… for one last time.

Pills in hand, I watched the sun's morning rays beaming through the windows onto the hardwood floor, and I listened as the sound of silence surrounded me.

Dishes were done, beds were made, and I was going through a mental list in my mind, making sure I didn't leave any loose ends and I had spoken to everyone I truly loved to say goodbye.

I was saddened, thinking about how much I would miss seeing my sons grow up; tears started rolling down my face. But I taught them well and knew they would be in good hands.

I pondered what it would be like never to wake up again and wondered what would be waiting for me on the other side.

I was ready to go, everything planned to perfection, and suddenly, the phone rang.

That was odd because my phone was always on silent. I looked over to see who it was, and it was someone from church whom I had only gotten to know because her son was friends with mine.

Why would she be calling? What did she want? Our sons haven't hung out together in over a year.

I picked up the phone and said, "Hello." She asked me to lead the betrayed women's support group at our church, and without hesitation, I immediately said No.

That part of my life was over, and I had moved on. I wasn't about to tell her my heart was shattered, my husband had left me, and I was getting ready to end it all, LOL!

She understood my position and then kindly asked me out to lunch to catch up.

I decided to meet her for lunch since she was aware of my "situation" and had supported me when I had attended the betrayed women's support group at the church.

I guess I won't be ending it all today.

The strangest thing happened to me in the days leading up to our lunch date.

I started seeing signs of overcoming porn addiction… one of the additional things I discovered about my husband in couple's counseling, along with his multiple affairs that occurred throughout half our marriage, an addiction to drugs, and a six-figure credit card debt that I happened to inherit when he left me.

A billboard sign on the side of the freeway read, "Are you addicted to porn?" and the URL address to get help. Even a colleague from an internet marketing group I was in mentioned how he overcame his addiction before marrying his wife.

What the hell?! Why would he volunteer that embarrassing tidbit of information?!

There were other signs, too, and I slowly wondered if God was trying to tell me something.

I met my friend for lunch. We caught up and chatted for a while. At the end of lunch, I asked if she found anyone to fill that position because I was considering it... only if it was still available.

Excitedly, she said it was and suggested I attend a social event the betrayed women had the next evening; that way, I could get to know them better.

I went, but by the end of the evening, I couldn't get out of that house fast enough!

The women were pleasant, and the conversations were cordial, but listening to each one of them giving me an account of their healing journey and how they were trying to restore their marriages made me feel like an outsider... a failure.

I became inundated with pain, triggered with flashbacks of my own discovery, and overwhelmed with feelings of inadequacy because my divorce was almost final.

What could these ladies possibly learn from me by leading this group?!

Choking back the tears, I said my goodbyes and said, "It was nice meeting all of you."

I got in my car, and before I could put the key in the ignition, tears flooded my eyes, and my freshly bandaged heart wounds were ripped wide open.

I was crying so hysterically I could barely see the road in the poorly lit neighborhood that I had to pull over.

Pain pierced my heart. I gripped the steering wheel and screamed in agony, "I can't go through this again!"

Just then, I heard a still, small voice whispering in my ear... "I've got you."

It was so clear and sounded so close that it startled me out of my crying. I turned my head to see who was there and heard it again... "I've got you."

I looked to the left, and I looked to the right and confirmed no one was there. I had always heard people talking about what God's voice sounded like. Was this it?!

Suddenly, a sense of peace and calm settled over me, and for the first time since my discovery, I KNEW everything would be okay.

That night, I made a promise with God. If this is what He wanted me to do, He would need to give me a faster path to healing.

I would be His voice and advocate for other women who were hurting from infidelity so they wouldn't have to go through what I went through... no one should have to go through what I went through because of heartbreak.

Today, I help betrayed women heal and move past the pain of infidelity in months instead of years so they can have peace and joy and live life as it was meant to be lived... happy, loved, and to the fullest.

About Sal Harper

Sal Harper is an Infidelity Recovery Specialist who experienced a "crisis" in her own marriage. She experienced first-hand the lies, deceit, and emotional trauma that infidelity & porn addiction took in her own marriage. On the other side, she found peace, love, joy, and a life filled with happiness and purpose.

Today, Sal is passionate about helping others heal and move past the pain of infidelity in months instead of years.

She offers her expertise inside her private "Beyond Infidelity" Facebook community and through her special events: "Fast-Track Your Healing" 5-Day Challenge, Live Tuesday Trainings, and Goddess Gatherings, a unique virtual dinner party experience.

Learn more and register for these special events by visiting: www.SalHarper.com.

"It is during our darkest moments that we must focus to see the light."

– ARISTOTLE ONASSIS

Broken to Glow

— Sandra Walsh —

I opened the trunk of my car, and immediately my heart sank. Where is it? OMG, please don't tell me it is gone... No, it has to be here! My heart got heavy, and my eyes began to tear up as I started shuffling through the bag of items from the Nursing Home that had belonged to my dad after he passed.

My dad wore hats, and he had some favorites. One of his favorites was a soft grey beanie I gave him for Christmas many years ago. I would remember to get him a new one every Christmas, but this particular one was his favorite.

As my dad got older, he began to get colder, so he would wear hats to keep his head warm. When he slept, he wore the beanie hat I gave him to keep his head warm. This past Christmas, my siblings and I decided to admit my dad into the Nursing Home after my mom passed away a year ago and his dementia worsened.

My dad was also suffering from Kidney failure. The doctors told us that he had about six months to live and would need 24-hour care, so we decided that being at the nursing home would be the best place for him, especially with 3 of the siblings living far away. We felt good about how they could keep him comfortable, and he would be in a safe environment.

All my life, all I wanted to do was to make my dad proud of me. At times, I felt like I was the little black sheep of the family. I did things my way and was always the adventurous one. He even nicknamed me "Road Packer," he would say, "Yep, that Sandy is the first one to get in the car and go somewhere."

It didn't matter where anyone was going; I wanted to go with them. Even as I got older, I would travel anywhere I wanted, even by myself. So, seeing my dad wear this hat daily made me feel a little bit accomplished. This sounds weird, but it was the simplest form of accomplishment.

I am the third child; I have two older brothers and a younger sister. I was the first daughter, and then, five years later, my sister came along. Having two older brothers, I was a little of a tomboy, and I had to make sure I did everything they did but better.

I was my dad's first "daddy's little girl," but then my sister came along and stole the show from me (haha)! Well, in my mind she did. She did nothing wrong but liked dolls and dresses; she was all girl.

So not only was I in competition with my brothers, but I was also in competition to keep my title as being daddy's little girl. So, I worked hard always to make my daddy proud. It seemed that I had to work harder at this than it did my sister. I'm sure she felt the same way, but I couldn't see that way.

With all that I accomplished in life, I never felt like I truly got the feeling of accomplishment from my dad. Yes, this was a lie from the devil; I know this now, but growing up, I always felt less than accomplished.

There was even this one time I asked for help from my dad to buy me some tires for my Jeep, and he told me no. He said, "Sandy, if I were to help you buy some tires for your Jeep, it would be like I approve of your lifestyle."

Wow, my lifestyle; at the time, I was 21 years old and had recently moved back in with them after getting divorced from a two-year marriage. I was finally exploring life a little, and he didn't approve of it.

As I was growing up, my dad sheltered us a lot. He didn't allow me to participate in school activities or go home with friends, and we were in church every time the doors were opened, so the first chance I got to get married, I did, even to someone I didn't love.

My dad sheltered us because when I was around 5 or 6, I was sexually abused by my uncle. My older brother found out my uncle was messing with me and told on him.

At the time, I felt mad at my brother for telling because that meant my daddy now knew what was going on, and he would be mad at me and not want me to be his little girl anymore because I was damaged.

Because of that, I felt punished. I wasn't allowed to do anything. I couldn't see that my dad felt horrible; he thought that he didn't protect me, so in his mind, he would protect me the only way he could by keeping me at home.

But I felt like I was being punished, and I had to try harder now to make him love me, be proud of me again, and be his little girl. So, I stayed home and was known as the sheltered girl at school.

That marriage was another failure and a disappointment to me and my dad (in my head, I felt like my dad was so disappointed in me), so when I divorced, I moved back in with them for a short period.

I felt like since I was 21, I could come and go as I pleased and explore everything I missed out on in high school, so yes, my lifestyle wasn't pleasing to him.

Later, I married a young man who saw no danger in life. He was full of adventure; he worked hard and played even harder. Shortly after getting married, we had two sons, and I quickly realized this man wasn't the one for me at all.

I thought I could change him, and he felt he could control me. I wanted more out of life; he wanted me to be like his mom and stay home, not be worldly.

After almost four years of marriage, we ended up getting divorced again. Yes, another failure in my daddy's eyes. Now, to try even harder to make him proud of me.

I wanted to go into the military but knew that I couldn't because I had two small boys to care for, so I decided to be a correctional officer at a prison.

My parents kept the boys for me to go to school for six weeks to get my certification. I passed, and for the first time, I felt a little accomplishment from my dad.

Then, about two years later, I met a man online, ran off, got married, and moved away with my boys after only knowing him for two weeks. Yep, another disappointment.

He lost his memory, I fell and broke my arm, and my parents had to come to get us and move us back home with them after only three months!!! So here I am with two small boys, no job, no house, no income, another divorce, a broken arm, and a heart full of failure and disappointment.

After healing from my broken arm, I returned to work at the prison and finally was on the right track. I was back in church and living right (according to my dad), met my husband (now of 20 years), and we got married.

My dad was happy again for me. I had finally done something right. I met a man who loved me and my boys like his own and even gave me a daughter. Even though I was striving now and doing well in my heart, I still felt like I was a disappointment, and I was still trying to make my daddy feel proud of me, so when I would see him wear this little beanie hat, it really meant the world to me.

When my dad passed, he had his beanie hat on; he also had the soft, silky pillow and the extra soft blanket I had given him. When he was admitted to the hospital, I had brought my silky pillow to use while staying with him before going into the nursing home.

He made mention of the pillow and said it sure does look soft, so I gave it to him. We all know hospital pillows aren't the most comfortable pillows. Knowing that he had my pillow as well made my heart smile because once I returned to Mississippi, I knew I wouldn't be able to see him as often as I wanted.

After my dad passed, I gathered his beanie hat, the silky pillow, and the soft blanket and put them into the trunk of my car. That evening, my husband made it to Georgia with my son and his family, and they took my car to use while in Georgia, and I would just ride back to Mississippi with him.

Five days have passed, and we are back in Mississippi. And I went to gather my dad's belongings out of my trunk. And there was no hat! I began to cry, and my heart began to feel evil.

It was a mad cry like I have never felt in my life. I was angry at myself, my son, and whoever took my dad's hat.

I wouldn't say I liked this feeling whatsoever, but it was there, and I had to do something about it. I called my son and asked him to look through his belongings to make sure it didn't get mixed up with their stuff or if it was left back in Georgia. It was confirmed no one had the hat or had seen it.

I was devastated.

I am not one to allow so many feelings into a piece of clothing as I did with this beanie hat. I had feelings like I had never felt before. I wanted to sleep, cry, and just give up because I lost a hat that meant so much to my dad.

I gave it to him; it kept him warm, and it was a piece of satisfaction knowing that I gave it to him, and he loved it. With it gone, I felt like I disappointed my dad and would never be able to make him proud of me again. I was almost willing to make everyone around me feel as horrible as I felt.

I could have made my son feel horrible about losing my dad's hat and let him see how it devastated me, but what would that have accomplished?

I could have closed up and shut down on the inside and eventually lost everything I had worked on to be successful. I could have even lost the joy I bring so many people daily, but I didn't.

I chose to live; I decided to let this sentimental hat go and hold on to the memory of how it gave my dad warmth and love, knowing I gave it to him.

It was like God said, "Sandy, don't let a material item steal your Joy and Love; don't be so selfish and destroy everything you have worked for over a missing hat."

So, then I cried, and I took out a piece of paper and started writing down all my feelings that I had been holding up over the years, and as I began to write, I didn't even realize I was holding on to so many feelings that were holding me hostage.

I started to feel relieved as I wrote each feeling out, which was a relief I needed. When I was done writing all my feelings out, I remembered hearing a podcast that sometimes you just needed to thank yourself, so I did.

I thanked God for using the loss of my dad's beanie hat to let loose my feelings so that I could move forward. You see, sometimes God allows bad things to happen to us so that we can be broken and glow brighter.

A few weeks passed, and my sister invited me and my brothers to Daytona Beach to spend a few days with her. This would be our first time together since our father passed.

My mom loved the beach, and my dad... well, he enjoyed staying in the room with the AC... lol. My dad loved my mom so much that he would always make a way to take us to the beach each year.

He worked every day out in the sun and heat, so his idea of going to the beach to sit in the sun wasn't really his cup of tea, but he did it anyway.

So, yes, I was very excited when my sister invited us to the beach.

As I was getting packed for the trip, I went out to my car to clean it out... as a Real Estate agent, I live out of my car... always on the run.

I had a bag of tools that included toilet paper, paper towels, cleaning supplies, measuring tape, water, and other items, so I decided to organize it and get the trash out.

As I go through the bag of items, you will never guess what I found... out of the blue... yes, I found my dad's hat. I was so excited I started jumping up and down and thought about all the hard feelings I originally had when I thought I had lost it.

It wasn't right that I blamed my son for losing it, so I immediately called him and asked for forgiveness. When I found it, I felt relieved and ashamed for putting so much emphasis on the hat.

It wasn't the hat, but I now realize that God allowed me to use his hat to get broken. That broken feeling allowed me to release so many emotions I had held inside that I couldn't move forward.

To be broken is a new birth… grace granted, and love endured.

About Sandra Walsh

Sandy Walsh is a mother of three, sassy to 5 grandchildren, and wife. Sandy moved to Bay Saint Louis, MS, from Georgia in 2017. After moving to MS, Sandy decided to start a career in Real Estate to meet people and learn about the area.

Sandy excelled very quickly in her Real Estate career by networking and putting herself out into the public eye. In 2021, Sandy finished the year in the top 1.5% of all agents in Mississippi at #33, and in 2022, Sandy ranked #13 in the State, top .5% in the US, and the top 1.5% in America's best. In 2023, Sandy and her husband opened their new brokerage, Allied Realty Coastal Homes, in Waveland. Before Real Estate, Sandy was a social worker and a Correctional Officer for the State of GA.

Sandy is involved in several Mardi Gras Krewes: Nereids, Iris, and Mystic Krewe of the SeaHorse a Pirate

Krewe, and Sandy was named Lady Claiborne II in 2022; Sandy enjoys participating in these events each year.

She enjoys working out, singing, walking, crafts, and hanging out with friends and family.

Learn more at www.alliedrealtycoastalhomes.com.

"Our deepest wounds carry the potential for the greatest healing; our cracks let the light in."

– UNKNOWN

Whatever You Want

Can Be Yours

— Shena Marie —

No one goes into a marriage expecting to be abused and dreaming of a terrible divorce, but sometimes, that is the reality of the situation. I remember the day I realized I was in an abusive marriage, and I had no choice but to take steps to escape like it was yesterday.

I watched the news that morning, and a woman and two children were missing. The father pleaded for their safe return, but something felt off to me.

I called my best friend and told her to turn on the news. I said I believed the family was dead and the dad had done it. She asked me how I knew, and I said I just did because that woman was just like me, and one day, my husband would kill me too.

That missing woman was Shannan Watts, and yes, her husband had killed her and their two young daughters. I still can't truly verbalize how I just knew, but that day changed the trajectory of my life. The realization that I would probably die one day, or my children could be killed with me somehow pushed me into action.

It may seem strange, but I didn't call the cops or file for divorce until over two years later. When I decided to leave, I had no money, credit, or job. My now ex and I owned a business together, but all of the assets were in his name, and all the debt was in mine. The fact that the state we were living in was not community property was something I failed to understand until it was too late.

I worked full-time in our business, raising two kids and doing everything around the house. He didn't even put his dishes in the sink or his laundry in the basket, but my desire to create money for myself and break free from the chains of that marriage was stronger than any need for sleep.

I started looking for work and found a commission-based recruiting job for a local insurance company. I had no experience or idea how to start, but I had the vision of something more and a desire that could not be quenched.

I would work after hours to get resumes and take recruiting calls while driving between construction estimates for the business. After a few months, I got the hang of it, and soon I was the top recruiter in my company. I told my ex that I was only paid monthly, even though it was twice a month, and put one of my paychecks in a separate account that he did not know of.

If you are in a situation where you need money, but it is too dangerous to be open about a second account, then this is the time to be sneaky. Get a job that has some cash involved and skim off the top. You could sell things online for extra bucks and put that in a separate account.

It is not easy, and I won't pretend it is, but it is so worth it to have the freedom and ability to leave when you need to and know that you can feed your kids no matter what.

I planned to save enough money to get a place for me and the kids and hire a great attorney. I knew my ex would cut us off when I left, and I wanted to be ready. There were many bumps in the road; hello, COVID-19, but I managed to save, and while I didn't have as much as I originally wanted, I still had enough to get us by when the time came.

In the winter of 2020, my ex became unbearable to deal with in the middle of the pandemic. He would force himself on me and threaten me almost daily. Once, when I refused my "wifely duty," he took all of my clothes, threw them down the stairs, and threw my shoes and shoe rack on top.

This destroyed many of my things and injured the stair railing and wall. He told me that if I had been a good wife and done what was necessary, then he would not have had to hurt my things. It got so bad that I was truly in fear for my life daily, and my best friend would call me every morning to ensure I was still alive. I couldn't sleep out of fear and would stay up until I couldn't keep my eyes open anymore because I was so afraid he would kill me when I was asleep.

I decided I couldn't wait any longer and started interviewing attorneys in the area. Two days before one of the interviews, my ex had called me the C-word and then was so mad that I was upset about it, he slammed my work computer to smithereens against my desk in a rage.

When I told the lawyer about this incident, he told me it was a crime and that I should call the police. That was the scariest phone call of my life, but it was also the best. I was taking back my life and future from the man stealing it. He was arrested, and over two years later, we have never been closer than 1,000 feet from one another.

The few days after finally getting my ex arrested for domestic violence and filing for divorce were a complete whirlwind. My kids were scared and had no idea what was going on.

My business was in upheaval because the two owners were not legally allowed to talk to one another. My finances were worse than I had planned for because not only had my ex cut me off like I knew he would, but he called all the bills I had paid for the previous three months and claimed they were fraudulent transactions.

Overnight, I had creditors breathing down my neck, and I was drowning in living expenses from months previous. I knew I was doing the right thing, but it did not feel like it then.

During mediation in divorce court, I gave up my interest in our very successful business for fractions of a penny on the dollar to get 85% custody of my children and protect them as much as possible. I went from being a millionaire to being destitute and on food stamps seemingly overnight.

They say it is not about getting knocked down but how you get up. In leaving an abusive marriage, I was allowed to truly find who I am and who I want to be for the first time in over a decade. I started to compete in pageants, and I have found my voice through pageantry. I can help others realize that they are in abusive situations and get tools and assistance to get out. No one should ever live in fear for their life, and I am on a mission to make sure that money is not why a woman stays.

Through divorce, I also lost my business and my job. I had been profit coaching on the side for years, even doing it for free for over five years, but I never really saw it as a business that could pay my bills.

I love being able to help business owners to understand their financial situation and have the empowerment to change it into something better. Once my divorce was finalized, my boyfriend encouraged me to try to make a real go of profit coaching as a business.

I am so glad he did because I wouldn't be where I am today without that encouragement. Sometimes, it takes someone seeing you from the outside looking in to know the truth, and for me, the fact was that I am a profit coach at heart.

It wasn't easy or simple to start over, but at least I knew that I knew what I was doing. You see, many years ago, the successful business I had just given up wasn't so successful.

On paper, we had a lot of sales, but the costs and overhead outpaced the income, and three years into the business, we could only pay ourselves 20k out of 500k in sales.

To add insult to injury, at the same time, we found out our accountant had been embezzling all of our tax money, and we owed the IRS over 70,000 dollars! I was broke and needed help finding where to turn. My ex, in his normal fashion, had said he wouldn't work any additional jobs, and I needed to "figure it out." So, figuring it out was what I did.

I took the entire next year to learn everything I could about taxes, business, costs, profits, etc. I re-did everything in the business that wasn't the sales. I negotiated with suppliers to get set rates for common items and marketed only the jobs I knew we could be profitable on.

I created budgets and timelines for every job, so we weren't spending additional labor or supply dollars where we didn't need to. My complete overhaul of the systems and processes in the business paid off, though, because we went from 4% profit to 25% profit in one year, and I was able to pay myself over 100k that year!

Once I had transformed my business, friends, and colleagues started asking how I did it and how they could, too. I started coaching out of a deep desire to help. I remember when I couldn't buy food or pay my mortgage, and I didn't want anyone else to feel how I had felt. I had many big wins with my pro bono clients during those years. It was great to see so many people win.

When I decided to go full-time into coaching, it was a natural progression from free coaching to having part-time clients to full-time. I have been blessed that within a year, I was able to create a six-figure business.

People always ask me how I did it and don't believe me when I tell them how simple it is. Simple is generally not easy, but it is simple anyway.

First, I started with a passion and a vision. I LOVE helping people make more money, and I am freaking good at it. I have yet to have a client fully implement my coaching and not have exponential results.

I have had clients go from broker than broke to over 250K in the bank in under one year. I had a client 4x her income in 4 months, and these are just a couple of the wins I am obsessed with.

My passion for my work is unwavering, and if you want to have a truly successful business that lights you up, your passion has to be the same.

Then you need vision. Where are you going?

What would it look like if you could paint a picture of your life and your business? You can go wherever you want, but the first step is to decide where that is.

So many people are unsuccessful or feel like they are spinning in circles because they lack direction. They lack direction because they haven't given it to themselves.

I have found that most people are afraid of their dreams. They feel too big or unreachable, but every mountain can be climbed with the correct planning and guidance.

Create a vivid vision for yourself to see who you must be to achieve it. Then, become that person and just take a little step every day.

Once you have the passion and vision, the rest is just strategy and execution. Take the vision and chunk it down into steps.

Where are you going to be in 3 years?

Where must you be in 1 year to make that 3-year plan possible? What must you do this quarter to make the year plan a reality?

What are the steps week-by-week for 13 weeks to achieve those quarterly goals?

Then, execute relentlessly.

So many people make it more complicated. They give themselves lists upon lists of extra things they "need" before they can start the real work.

When I started my coaching business, for real, I had a splash page, some business cards, and a great 30-second commercial. Everything else infrastructure-wise has come after, with time, planning, and as I have truly needed it.

This is why having a coach is so crucial. A great coach can help you decide the best next step and how to execute. They can keep you on track and moving toward your goals and vision at all times. They can also ensure you don't get distracted by the shiny objects that seemingly come from everywhere and will derail you from what you want to achieve.

This is why I love being a coach so much. I help people realize what has always been there, what my clients could do but weren't. Whether it be helping someone make enough profit to buy their partner a Christmas gift for the first time or helping a multi-million-dollar company double their revenue and triple their profitability in one year.

Whatever you want, it can be yours. Grab your passion, create your vision, strategize your plan, and execute like never before. Never let anyone tell you that you can't and keep going no matter what. If you need support, my inbox is always open.

About Shena Marie

I have been there...selling a lot, but completely overwhelmed and feeling stuck on a hamster wheel of sales and bills, then sales and bills. I never seemed to be able to get ahead and the more I grew my sales, the more I seemed to grow all of my issues and workload too. I knew that SOMETHING had to give. I dreamed of financial freedom and vacations, not continual 1am work nights and fretting about payroll.

This is when I decided to change the way I was doing business AFTER the sale, and then everything changed. I went from the struggle bus to a profitable 7-figure entrepreneur. Now I know how to effectively scale in business, make great income, and have the lifestyle I've always dreamed of.

Using the techniques that have worked in my business and my client's businesses I want to help you to turn your business from an anxiety inducing, never ending pile of work, to the profitable, well-oiled machine organization you always dreamed it could be. Let's create your perfect profit picture together and take you from dismal work to dream life! Learn more at www.yourpocketcfo.com.

"Never apologize for being a warrior, for every battle scars only make you shine brighter."

– NIKKI ROWE

Shining Brightly

— Tina Torres —

In the depths of despair, one force can truly lift you up: God. Let me take you back to over four years ago when I found myself in a dark and debilitating depression. It was a place of unimaginable pain and loneliness, where I felt like giving up on life itself. Night after night, I pleaded with God to take away my anguish and release me from the hurt that consumed me. I was lost and abandoned, and my spirit was shattered.

Recently, I went through a difficult divorce after a toxic 20-year marriage with a narcissistic, alcoholic partner who repeatedly betrayed me. One would think that finally breaking free would bring me newfound love and happiness, but it didn't.

I longed to return to him, trapped in a trauma-bonded relationship with nowhere else to turn. To add to my distress, I lost a well-paying six-figure job, my only source of income. It was my first corporate role, and although I wasn't passionate about it, I excelled.

The very next day, my youngest son, at the tender age of 18, left for basic training as he made the selfless decision to join the United States Army. As a mother of three, my primary identity had always been that of a devoted mom. With my son gone, I felt adrift, no longer a wife, and not knowing who I was outside of my role as a mother.

I moved to a new town where I knew no one and took temporary refuge with family members I hadn't lived with since my teenage years. But even they turned their backs on me when I needed their support the most.

In this moment of heartbreak, I found myself completely alone and desperate for guidance. Yes, I had God on my side, or so I thought. However, as the days turned into weeks, I sank even deeper into the abyss of my despair.

In my darkest moments, friends tried to help me, but their assistance only felt degrading. They belittled my capabilities and what I could bring to the table, knowing full well that I was desperate for money.

After 90 days of submerging in this suffocating depression, I reached a breaking point. I begged God to end my life, and one night, I swallowed a bottle of sleeping pills. I left letters for my children and a lengthy note to my ex-husband, meticulously planning my exit.

Tearfully, I drifted off to a tortured sleep, only to awaken the next morning, still alive. Frustrated and full of anger, I screamed at God. I couldn't escape the overwhelming pain and hurt that plagued me. But that day, God spoke to me with unwavering clarity. He told me that it was not yet my time to leave this earth, that I was here for a purpose. The onus was on me to discover what that purpose entailed.

The following morning, God planted a seed in my heart. He prompted me to start writing in a gratitude journal. Every day, I would jot down everything I was grateful for, no matter how small. It could be as simple as the warmth of the sun or the comforting presence of my two dogs snuggled beside me.

I faithfully followed this practice for 90 consecutive days while simultaneously doing whatever it took to earn money. I owe a debt of gratitude to services like Uber Eats, DoorDash, and Instacart, which helped keep my finances afloat. I hustled, working early mornings, late nights, weekends, and even holidays to make ends meet. Some months were incredibly challenging, and I struggled to pay rent on my modest one-bedroom trailer. Despite the hardships, I persisted.

During my journey, I was fortunate to find a supportive community that guided and encouraged me. Inspired by a powerful vision, I embarked on a mission to write my own book - a gratitude journal designed to positively impact millions of individuals, particularly women, by starting their day with gratitude.

On an auspicious day, March 17th, I officially launched my book. However, fate had a surprising turn in store for me - as the world went into quarantine, disrupting life as we knew it.

I found myself in San Diego, California, amidst a photo shoot, when news reached me that my book had not only made it to the best-seller lists but had reached the esteemed position of number one in three different categories across seven countries. My dream had become a reality - I was now a renowned and accomplished best-selling author.

But in the face of this incredible success, a question loomed: What next? Excitement should have filled the air with 18 speaking engagements scheduled over the next six months. However, cancellations began pouring in, one after another, due to the pandemic.

In this moment of uncertainty, an idea sparked within me - I decided to launch a morning talk show alongside a dear friend. The purpose was simple yet profound: to bring a glimmer of positivity to the start of each day for individuals burdened by negativity, negative thoughts, and pessimistic ideas.

Over two years, our talk show became a platform through which we interviewed over 500 remarkable entrepreneurs. Many of these individuals were cherished connections from my 20-year journey in the marketing business.

Through the show, I rekindled these relationships and established myself as a social media manager and creative director for numerous businesses and companies. It was a whirlwind adventure as I traveled the globe, assisting these entities in crafting unique and standout brand identities.

Together, we sought to make a lasting difference in the lives of others, empowering them to shine amidst the world's noise. I spent 2 1/2 years traveling to 48 cities, immersing myself in new experiences. But the toll it took on my well-being was undeniable.

Energy depletion, mental fog, and sleeplessness became my daily struggles. In my quest for answers, I discovered a hidden danger lurking within me: stage four adrenal fatigue. Completely unaware of this deadly disease, I confronted the urgent need to prioritize my health.

Following my doctor's advice, I made the difficult decision to reduce my travels and take much-needed time off. While this choice impacted my business, it also sparked a new opportunity. I found solace in supporting other women, entrepreneurs, and coaches in writing their own best-selling books.

It was a venture I could undertake from the comfort and safety of my own home. Thus, I embarked on a journey to empower women, helping them reach the coveted title of number one best-selling author.

So far, I've guided 32 women to achieve this remarkable feat in various categories across multiple countries. The success of these women inspired me to create a comprehensive package, enabling others to replicate their triumphs.

Amid this transformative period, a particular moment crystalized the essence of my mission. During a show, someone referred to me as a glowstick. The words resonated deeply. To shine brightly, like a glowstick, sometimes we must endure the breaking process.

Adversity and circumstances beyond our control may dim our glow, but the potential for unparalleled radiance lies within that struggle. With this profound insight, the idea for a collaboration book took shape in my mind. I aptly named it "Be a glowstick Girl," symbolizing the strength and resilience necessary for our brightest glow to emerge.

Have you ever considered how much we can learn from a humble glowstick? It may seem odd, but there's something profound about the way it works.

A glowstick does not start shining until it's broken.

It reinforces the idea that sometimes, to shine truly, we must undergo a transformation of our own. Just like a glowstick, we often need to step out of our comfort zones, face challenges, and embrace change before radiating our brightest light.

Imagine that glowstick sitting on the store shelf, waiting to fulfill its purpose. It remains inert, motionless, and unassuming. It's only when someone grasps it, bends it, and breaks it that the magic happens.

Suddenly, the chemistry inside the glowstick is set into motion, and a brilliant luminescence emerges slowly. It's as if the glowstick is telling us that sometimes, the moments of breaking can be the catalyst for our greatest transformations. It reminds us that our challenges and hardships can ultimately lead to our growth and the unleashing of our true potential.

But what does it mean for us to "shine brightly"? To me, it means living a life that is authentic, fulfilling, and impactful. It means pursuing our passions, embracing our uniqueness, and radiating positivity.

Like the glowstick's glow, our brightness can bring joy, inspiration, and even light to those around us. So, the next time you feel like life is breaking you, remember the remarkable journey of a glowstick. Embrace the discomfort, welcome the changes, and let yourself shine brilliantly in the face of adversity.

About Tina Torres

Tina Torres is a force to be reckoned with in the book writing and publishing industry. With a proven track record of success, she has established herself as one of the most sought-after self-publishing experts in the business. As the CEO and Founder of Pink Door Marketing Agency, Tina has helped countless writers navigate the often-complicated world of book publishing, from writing and editing to marketing and promotion.

In addition to her work as a marketing expert, Tina is also a highly respected author in her own right. Her books, The Gratitude Journal and Beyond Gratitude, have both achieved #1 bestseller status, earning Tina the recognition of being a two-time bestselling author. Her books are a testament to her passion for helping others, as they provide practical tools and insights for cultivating gratitude and positivity in everyday life.

Tina's expertise and lived experience have made her a sought-after coach and speaker as well. She has been recognized as a Woman of Influence by Success Magazine for her outstanding contributions to the industry. She is a talk show host and a global speaker, inspiring audiences around the world with her message of positivity, resilience, and self-empowerment.

Tina is based in Atlanta, Georgia, where she lives with her family. She is a firm believer in the power of gratitude, and she is committed to living an attitude of gratitude herself. Through her work, Tina is helping to transform the lives of countless individuals, empowering them to share their own stories and create a lasting impact in the world. Whether you're a seasoned writer or a first-time author, Tina Torres is the expert you need to take your book to the next level.

Learn more about Tina and Pink Door Marketing at www.gratitudespecialist.com.

"A diamond is a piece of coal that handled stress exceptionally well."

– UNKNOWN

I Chose to Soar

— Tyla Lusk —

When asked to share my story, I initially hesitated because I have always been a private person. However, my love for people and my joy in spending time with them is balanced by my need for solitude to find inner calm.

It has taken me some time to realize that I am an empath, greatly influenced by the energy of those around me. Whether energy givers or energy suckers surround me determines the course of my week. Can anyone else relate?

Depending on the company I keep, I either hum with creative energy or retreat to restore my own. While I have valuable insights to share with others, I also cherish the tranquility of my personal space. Living my dream life on what I affectionately call my "compound" nourishes my spirit.

This name originated when it was nothing more than a distant dream, but now it is the place I proudly call home—a testament to the blend of hard work, tears, and aspirations that have brought me here. Although I hadn't planned on sharing how I arrived at this point, I feel compelled to do so.

Creating beauty has always been an integral part of my identity. It is one of those God-given gifts that come naturally, flowing from the depths of my soul.

I always loved painting, singing, and unleashing my creativity from a young age. Writing and daydreaming were among my favorite pastimes, while athleticism was not my strong suit. I embraced my girly side, which remains evident today, although my favorite color has evolved to black for its versatility. Yet, I won't pass up a touch of hot pink or leopard print to accentuate the black. And a touch of sparkle? Yes please!

Becoming an entrepreneur was never part of my conscious plan, although, in hindsight, it was destined to be. I witnessed my parents tirelessly build remarkable businesses, which consumed their lives. I didn't want that for myself.

I sought a "normal" existence—a life where I could create beautiful, dazzling things, enjoy every moment, and return home to my family with a steady paycheck.

Freshly married, I worked in retail, excelling but lacking fulfillment. One day, my husband asked me what I truly wanted. Without hesitation, I expressed my wish to attend beauty school and become a nail tech.

He asked me why? to which I confidently replied that I felt it was my purpose in the world at that time. Moreover, the flexibility of setting my schedule was definitely preferable to the demanding hours of retail.

Nails had always captivated me; it was the ultimate embodiment of femininity, immersed in polishes and glitter, making everyone sparkle and shine. In 1996, I took a leap of faith and got my license, embarking on a journey that would lead me to establish a thriving nail business over the next few decades.

While it was far from easy, and I even considered quitting several times during the first year when daycare expenses nearly eclipsed my income, I eventually found my rhythm. My client base grew steadily, and a couple of years later, I expanded my services to include permanent makeup—a venture that brought me immense joy. Business was booming, and life was wonderful.

Then came 2001—a year that shattered the bliss I had known. I was a mother to one beautiful daughter, eagerly awaiting the arrival of our second child. Little did I know that our anticipation would be met with heartbreak. Our second daughter was stillborn, turning what should have been a joyous time into the darkest chapter of our lives.

It was a shocking, unimaginable loss that continues to haunt me, even after 22 years. We struggled to comprehend the magnitude of our devastation as if trapped in an endless, horrific nightmare. The weeks and months that followed altered the course of my life forever.

Despite the weight of my grief, I had to return to work. Bills had to be paid, life had to move forward, and my surviving daughter needed me. Amid my sorrow, I discovered something profound—nothing could ever compare to the pain I had just endured.

Nothing could be as terrifying or as devastating. Nothing I pursued in life would be as harrowing as that experience. This realization sparked a transformation within me. I resolved to live without regrets, to seize every opportunity, and to create with abandon.

God granted me the strength and resilience to move forward, to emerge from the depths of despair, and to allow that tragedy to shape me for the better. Along this journey, I have encountered others who have gone through similar ordeals. Some have allowed their experiences to mold them into stronger individuals, while others have drowned in their grief.

I chose not to drown.

Remember, I am a creator. That is my gift—a constant influx of ideas that I struggle to distill into a singular focus. I don't claim that all my ideas would have been profitable, but they filled my mind to the brim. During those challenging times, I prayed fervently for clarity on my myriad of creative, seemingly crazy ideas.

One concept had been shelved years ago due to life's demands and limited resources. I often quipped to my friends about inventing something and appearing on QVC to make millions.

I did embark on that path, but it took some time to figure it all out. From that grief and life-altering experience, my journey as a multi-preneur began.

I bid farewell to my job and opened my first salon, which thrived and continues to do so. Amid it all, I birthed my very first creation—my Franken Creation, as I jokingly call it. I felt like Dr. Frankenstein, exclaiming, "It's alive!" when I saw the first sample.

The excitement was palpable. I was doing everything and anything! Even if it was a colossal flop, I refused to live a life consumed by "what ifs." And thus, my marvelous Tigerlily Interchangeable Sandals came into existence.

They were born out of grief from the depths of my heart. As a self-professed shoe lover, I now run a shoe company—what could be better? (And it's grown far beyond what I could've imagined.)

I take immense pride in my creation. I have poured my soul into this endeavor, from conceiving the idea to designing each style, bringing them to market, and patenting them.

For context, the journey from concept to product spanned over two years, and it took an additional twenty-two months to secure the patent. None of this would have been possible without the unwavering support of my incredible husband of 27 years, Jeff.

We now run our companies together—he manages logistics and wholesale accounts while I focus on product development, creativity, and collaborating with our amazing clients and friends, creating products to bring their unique brands to life.

Our products have graced the shelves of QVC, national department stores, and thousands of boutiques and spas across the country.

This crazy business venture has also led me to explore other product ideas, face failures, and gain invaluable experience in overseas sourcing, product development, and design.

Some years ago, as a favor, I began assisting friends in designing and developing physical products for their brands, inadvertently giving birth to yet another business.

Word spread and more relationships were forged. Before I knew it, I spent most of my time bringing others' ideas to fruition, and I have loved every minute.

It was an unexpected turn, but my genuine love, care, and passion for creating and sourcing functional and fabulous products fueled this venture. I find tremendous joy in utilizing my gifts and experience to streamline designing, importing, and creating custom-branded products for other businesses or brands seeking to enhance their sales and brand strategy.

Thanks to the years of experience and trusted relationships I have cultivated, I have access to incredible resources for custom manufacturing with the highest standards of quality and excellence.

My goal is to assemble all the pieces that make your brand shine through in your products, delivering uniqueness and functional and fabulous custom products to your customers.

I discovered that more than my own ideas, I derive immense satisfaction from helping others bring their visions to life. I am deeply invested in what I do.

Collaborating with clients to make their dreams a reality, hand in hand with their brand, is both exhilarating and rewarding.

Furthermore, I can even guide clients through creating their own products, navigating the winding road with them until they, too, can proudly create their unique offerings.

Through the incredible opportunities afforded to us by this remarkable business, my husband and I were able to purchase our dream property—a sprawling acreage where we have been building our dream life.

On this land, we now grow a significant portion of our own food, with a vegetable garden and what we affectionately call the "food forest," that currently has 55 fruit trees and counting on the other side of the property.

Considering my history as a former plant killer, this is quite the achievement for me. I am always learning and growing. We love our life and have deep gratitude for the pivotal moments that have shaped us, strengthened us, and helped us appreciate our family and life even more.

We went on to have an incredible son, now in college, and our sweet daughter has found a wonderful husband, the kind any mother would wish for.

Knowing what I know now, I am grateful for the journey, despite its challenges. It has forged a strength within me that I never thought possible. We are all capable of living our dream lives.

If I had allowed my trauma to define me, to engulf me, my family would have missed out on the life we now share, and all the people I have the privilege to create with, and help would have missed out as well.

Always remember, it is your choice whether to soar or to fall. I chose to soar, and you can too.

About Tyla Lusk

Meet Tyla Lusk, the unstoppable CEO of Tigerlily Creations LLC, whose vibrant creativity and entrepreneurial spirit have left an indelible mark on the beauty industry. With over 27 years of experience, Tyla has forged a reputation as a leading professional permanent makeup artist, designer, inventor, importer, and multi-business owner based in Southwest Florida.

Known as the "Queen of Bling," Tyla's passion for designing and sourcing fabulous yet functional products set her apart from the crowd. Her innovative creations include the patented Tigerlily Interchangeable Sandals, TLC Show-Off Bag, Diva Defense Pepper Spray, and an array of other sought-after products. These extraordinary items have graced the shelves of national department stores, QVC, boutiques, salons, and spas nationwide.

Tyla's expertise extends beyond her own product line, as she collaborates closely with large companies, lending her artistic touch to design and source products for their unique brands. Her innate ability to breathe life into personalized brand visions has made her an invaluable asset to businesses seeking to elevate their revenue and market presence through custom-branded products.

With a keen eye for quality and excellence, Tyla has meticulously built relationships with top-tier vendors and manufacturers worldwide. Her wealth of experience in importing and designing has honed her ability to curate the finest textiles and materials, resulting in products that exude the highest standards of craftsmanship.

For Tyla, integrating personal brands into products is the key to unlocking limitless growth opportunities. In the digital age of social media and online marketing, connecting with customers on a personal level has become paramount. By infusing brands into custom-designed merchandise, Tyla believes in creating a magical connection between businesses and their customers that resonates long after the purchase is made.

While Tyla adores crafting her own Tigerlily line, she finds true joy in helping others bring their creative ideas and customized items to life. Passionate about supporting small businesses, she actively assists entrepreneurs in navigating the process of designing, importing, and manufacturing unique products that reflect their brand essence.

If you would like to connect with Tyla, contact her at www.TylaLusk.com.

"Sometimes the most beautiful people are beautifully broken."

– ROBERT M. DRAKE

The Pendulum Swing

— Wendy Lee —

You know, there's this one scripture that has been my absolute favorite - James 1:2-4. It says, "Consider it pure joy when you face trials of various kinds because you know that the testing of your faith produces perseverance. Let perseverance finish its work so that you may be mature and complete, not lacking anything."

Now, why would a verse about facing trials hold such a special place in my heart? Well, let me tell you what I've come to understand through my life's journey - growth doesn't happen in the simple seasons. It's not during the easy times that we truly evolve. Instead, it's when we're faced with trials and find ourselves amidst life's refining fires.

Oh, I've had my share of trials, especially in recent years, but then again, we all have, haven't we? I resonate so deeply with that scripture from James because it acknowledges trials of "various" or "many" kinds.

Some trials just hit us out of nowhere, completely beyond our control. Others, well, I admit, we might bring upon ourselves. Regardless of their origin, though, we have the power to view them through a lens of joy.

You see, we have a choice. I could see these trials as malevolent forces out there to get and destroy me. But I've decided to look at them differently - as opportunities to be built up, refined, renewed, molded, and matured. It's like walking through a transformative fire that purges away the impurities and leaves behind a stronger, brighter version of ourselves.

So, my friend, as we share the incredible stories of women who have faced their brokenness, only to rise again, shining brighter than ever, remember the wisdom of James' scripture. Let's journey together through inspiring tales of resilience, and I hope they ignite a spark of hope and empowerment within you, just as they have within me.

Forty-two years old and twice divorced. What a failure. This isn't what I planned as a kid. When I was young, I dreamed of having a beautiful family one day – The dream guy, the perfect home, and four fun and smart kids.

We'd never worry about money, travel the world together, and my marriage would be pure romance. Ha!

Married the first time at age 18 because "we had to make it right before the Lord" - two kids, alcoholism, infidelity, partying, blowing money, buying our first house, college, full-time work, and several rounds of marriage counseling.

He was the alcoholic – I was the unfaithful one. Trials – ones I brought on myself. At age 27, I found someone who paid attention to me and my kids. I left. Divorced. I remarried within two years. I was broken, insecure, surrounded by people I should have been able to look up to – but they were all broken and insecure as well.

Second marriage. Still broken. Still insecure. But this guy – this one, I could build a life with. He loved my kids. My ex was never around. Stepdad stepped in full force. Y'all know the drill if you've been married.

Marriage is hard. Trials. But we were happy. Mostly. I was insistent that we communicate, always. But he didn't. So eventually, I didn't. Our life became about our kids. We had two from my first marriage, had two together, and adopted three from Africa – one with cerebral palsy. People thought we were heroes. I had a big online presence, and outside looking in, we were perfect, godly, and happy.

Twenty-twenty was a hell of a year for everyone. But for me, the pandemic was the least of my issues. That year, I lived my worst nightmare, and the trials hit one after another for the next two years. I'm not going to bore you with all the details. But the quick run-down is this:

My 2-year-old baby girl was molested by the oldest boy I brought into my home by adoption – my worst nightmare came true – and it happened under my nose when I should have known better.

My friend's husband murdered a man in front of her.

My cousin's wife took her life and left behind four kids. Our special needs daughter was in and out of the hospital – vomiting sometimes eight times a day - tube feedings – medications - and doctor visits.

One of my kids was doing drugs and running away from home.

My Facebook account (where I ran my whole business) was shut down completely and never restored - I had to start over.

My mother physically assaulted me in my grandmother's front yard because I didn't answer her phone call.

My oldest biological kid went off to college.

We moved away from the only town I had lived in since 2002.

Another son went off to college, then a few months in, was arrested and kicked out of school – bail money, attorney fees, heartache, stress.

My marriage was falling apart.

I lost a dear friend to suicide.

I spent too much money.

My husband wasn't working.

All the stress was on me to provide.

I was building three businesses.

Trials. Trials. Trials.

I was done. I was exhausted.

At the same time that ALL of that was happening, I was growing my coaching business:

I launched a business with my financial services firm.

I grew my new Facebook page to over 58K followers.

I hired a business coach.

I had my highest revenue year.

I started going to therapy.

I took time to heal.

I made some hard decisions.

One of those hard decisions was another divorce.

It was September of 2021. I was driving to a leadership retreat in Destin, Florida, for my network marketing business. I was going alone, meeting with about 12 other leaders I had never met. On that 6-hour drive, I spent much time in quiet thought. Life had been SO noisy and stressful that it was nice just to be.

Most describe me as an outgoing person. I have a bubbly personality, not a shy bone in my body, and unafraid to step on stages and speak or sing.

But, when it came to small groups of people I didn't know, I would always retreat - get quiet - go into my shell - and observe until I felt that those around me wouldn't judge the real me.

I grew up with a mom who would always tell me that girls would be mean to me because they were jealous, and boys would be mean to me because they liked me.

What that said to my subconscious is:

"If you are pretty, smart, AND show a fun personality, everyone will be mean to you."

And honestly, it paralyzed me more than I realized. I suppressed the real me and became a lesser version of myself to be liked.

But on that drive, I made a decision.

"I'm 41 years old," I told myself.

"It's time to be the real you, regardless of what others think. It's time to live. It's time to be authentic. No more pretending or hiding."

It took about 3 of those 6 hours to think through what it means to show up as the real me.

So, I did it.

I ripped all the walls down before walking in that door. When I walked into that mansion on the beach, I greeted every person in the place with hugs, excitement for the weekend, and my full-on bubbly personality.

Immediately, I felt free.

The second day there, we had a photographer scheduled to come in. My friend Nadya (who owned the house with her husband and my upline leader, John) put me in charge of ensuring we got great photos with the photographer.

My most immediate feeling was "me?" ... But I embraced it. I was a goofball behind the camera to help the one in front of the camera laugh and get comfortable.

I gave verbal affirmation, telling the girls how beautiful they were, and I had an absolute blast. When it was my turn for photos, instead of feeling awkward (like I usually did), I acted like no one was watching!

I jumped up on the pool's edge and laughed, twirled, kicked, and had a freaking blast. To this day, one of the photos from that photography session is the best photo I've ever taken.

It is a photo that represents the REAL me. That trip was a turning point in my life. Oh, and I have to say this – I don't think everyone from that trip liked me by the end of the weekend. But I am completely ok with it - because I was me.

My day returning from that trip was when I decided my marriage was over. I walked through the doors, ran to my husband, who was out back cooking dinner on the grill, and started talking with excitement about how incredible my weekend was and how freeing it was to be fully me.

He turned around and looked at me with pure irritation and said, "You just walked in the door. Can you calm down and give me a minute?"

That big, bubbly, happy woman was shrunk down to nothing. I know that may not seem like a big deal to you reading this, but in that moment, all the feelings of not being enough or too much and insecurity swept over me like a flood.

I walked into my laundry room, shut the door, took a deep breath, and said, "I'm done. I'm done changing who

I am to fit what someone else wants. I'm done having happiness drained from me. I'm done not being me."

Now, was that one situation a reason to leave a marriage? Of course not. But it was the final straw. Now, hear this – I made plenty of mistakes in my marriage. I don't blame him. I also don't think you should blame me for this. I blame brokenness and lack of communication.

The next year and a half of my life was like a constant pendulum swing from the most exhilarating and happy times to the most broken and devastating. But I'll tell you this. Every single trial was a blessing. Every single trial taught me something.

I have learned what boundaries look like. I have learned how to control my reaction to my emotions. I have learned how to see myself as a daughter of God. I have learned how to truly forgive (and the hardest person to forgive was myself). I have learned to listen more deeply, speak up more often, and love without expectations.

I have learned what it feels like to be a daughter of God.

Everything I worked SO hard to build felt like they were all falling apart. But I'm here to tell you – they weren't. The brokenness didn't kill me, didn't ruin me, didn't break me. It built me up.

Jim Rohn said, "The same wind blows on us all: the winds of disaster, opportunity, and change. Therefore, it is not the blowing of the wind, but the setting of the sails that will determine our direction in life."

I took the brokenness, mistakes, and lessons learned and let them fuel me. Over the few months post-divorce, the Lord took me through such a journey of trusting Him and forgiving myself. It was a beautiful experience. Now, I have clarity like never before, and I believe I am truly on the path God laid for me. NOTHING was on accident. Nothing was for nothing.

Be a victim of the brokenness and hurt that comes at you in life, OR let the trials bring you joy and make you shine. You get to choose.

So, if you're struggling right now or going through a trial that you feel is just too much, or maybe those winds of life keep hitting you over and over, and over, I want to leave you with a few things that I used to help me get through and shine bright.

First, remember that "this too shall pass." All pain is temporary, and with time, all circumstances can improve. Remind yourself of this in the midst of the storm.

Secondly, put your trust in God. You may not be a believer, but I'll tell you, I don't know how anyone makes it through this life without drawing to God. I know that He is my source, always. He is a loving Father that would never leave his daughter out in the cold. The words of the Bible show me that He provided for His children throughout the world's history, and He will provide for me. When the overwhelm comes, I remind myself that I can trust Him.

Next, surround yourself with people that will push you to glow up instead of being beaten down. Don't surround yourself with those that want to have a pity party with you. Be around those who empathize but encourage you to keep growing and turn things around.

Finally, know your vision. Where do you want to be at the end of this earthly life? Whose lives do you want to impact? What experiences do you want to have? Get SO clear on your vision that nothing will stop you from pursuing it.

Count it joy, my friend, whenever you face hard times. Because that is your sign that you're one step closer to becoming the woman you need to be to achieve all you're called to achieve.

About Wendy Lee

Wendy Lee, a mom of 6 living in Chattanooga, Tennessee, is a digital entrepreneur and content creator known for her work in the online business and marketing space.

With over ten years of experience as a Network Marketing Leader and Coach, she recognized a gap in the coaching industry: the need for more financial education for network marketers.

Through her own journey of understanding finances, Wendy launched a financial coaching agency with the Turning Point Group. Her mission is to teach network marketers how to grow their income, manage their money, and multiply it - creating generational wealth.

Wendy is passionate about helping others achieve financial freedom and financial abundance - Live More and Give More.

Learn more at www.turningpnt.org.

About Tina Torres

Tina Torres is a force to be reckoned with in the book writing and publishing industry. With a proven track record of success, she has established herself as one of the most sought-after self-publishing experts in the business. As the CEO and Founder of Pink Door Marketing Agency, Tina has helped countless writers navigate the often-complicated world of book publishing, from writing and editing to marketing and promotion.

In addition to her work as a marketing expert, Tina is also a highly respected author in her own right. Her books, The Gratitude Journal and Beyond Gratitude, have both achieved #1 bestseller status, earning Tina the recognition of being a two-time bestselling author. Her books are a testament to her passion for helping others, as they provide practical tools and insights for cultivating gratitude and positivity in everyday life.

Tina's expertise and lived experience have made her a sought-after coach and speaker as well. She has been recognized as a Woman of Influence by Success Magazine for her outstanding contributions to the industry. She is a talk show host and a global speaker, inspiring audiences around the world with her message of positivity, resilience, and self-empowerment.

Tina is based in Atlanta, Georgia, where she lives with her family. She is a firm believer in the power of gratitude, and she is committed to living an attitude of gratitude herself. Through her work, Tina is helping to transform the lives of countless individuals, empowering them to share their own stories and create a lasting impact in the world. Whether you're a seasoned writer or a first-time author, Tina Torres is the expert you need to take your book to the next level.

Learn more about Tina and Pink Door Marketing at www.gratitudespecialist.com.

Share Your Glow-Up!

With the success of Be a Glowstick Girl, Pink Door Marketing is proud to announce the launch of a second edition of Be a Glowstick Girl, a collaboration book project where you can purchase a chapter to share your story with the world.

With this package, you'll get 2,500 words to truly express yourself and your experiences. You'll also receive an author page including your headshot, bio and social media handles, as well as a call to action to help promote your message.

Not only that, but you'll be part of a best-selling book and meet 20 amazing women that you'll be friends with for a lifetime. You'll be able to exchange ideas and stories, and you'll receive 12 weeks of group coaching to help you with your writing and marketing strategy.

And the best part? All marketing, media sheets, editing and formatting will be taken care of for you! You can focus on sharing your message with the world while we handle the details behind the scenes.

Don't miss out on this incredible opportunity to share your story and join a powerful community of women. If you're interested in learning more, just reply to this email and we'll send you all the details.

Are you ready to share your Glowstick Girl story? Kick things off with your first coaching call at www.bit.ly/3EPGxw1.

Take Charge of Your Dreams and Become a Bestselling Author!

Tina Torres has created the 120 Days to Bestseller Program to help you take charge of your dreams in becoming a bestselling author. In 120 days, you'll write your book, market it, and publish it — all in one program!

There's still time to finish your book by the end of next quarter, and we invite you to sign up now, so you can take advantage of every minute of your bestseller journey of getting your book written and published!

In 120 days, you'll write your book, market it, and publish it — all in one program! Having a popular book on Amazon means:

You can bring in major traffic on demand – Amazon is the #6 website in the world (#3 in the USA) and has a lot of buyers to send your way…

You get to increase your credibility and be seen as an expert in your field…

You can use your "bestselling author" badge on cover photos, blogs, business cards, and speeches, giving you a real edge in the marketplace…

TAKE A LOOK INSIDE…

In the 120 Days to Bestseller Coaching Program, we'll work together to develop an in-depth revision plan through sixteen weeks of personalized prompts, assignments, and weekly one-on-one coaching calls.

Publishers typically have strict requirements for how manuscripts must be formatted for submission. If your book is going to get the attention it deserves, it will have to meet those standards precisely. That's why Editing, Formatting, and Publishing are all included.

The best marketing campaigns succeed because they are carefully crafted for individual authors and titles. It means diving in and getting to know the work — in the 120 Days to Bestseller Program; I'll show you how to promote to both readers and the media.

Your story has the power to shape our world, but here's the problem. Nobody knows that it exists! We're here to take care of that part as well.

WHAT YOU'LL GET

- Step-by-Step Expertise, Guidance, Marketing, and Resources to Make It Big!
- Weekly Coaching and Accountability Calls
- Market Research
- Professionally Designed Book Cover
- Sizzle Reel
- Email Campaigns
- Publishing Start to Finish
- Editing and Formatting
- Social Media and Marketing Campaigns

Ready to Get Started?

Are you ready to take charge of your dreams and become a bestselling author? Kick things off with your first coaching call at https://bit.ly/3EPGxw1.

Writing Resources

Get The 10 Steps to Becoming a Best-Selling Author Guide

(go.120daystobestseller.com)

Everyone has a story…

But the difference is that YOU have a story worth reading about.

Now it's time to dig it up, and write it down, because that story that got you to where you are today? It's going to make you a best-selling author.

Tina's "10 Steps to Becoming a Bestseller" guide will show you exactly how to achieve your best seller dreams in just 4 short months.

Inside, you'll discover:

- Step by Step guide on how to write YOUR story.
- How to craft a compelling and engaging story that makes others want to work with YOU!

- The importance of having a strong branding and marketing plan.
- Tips for effective editing and formatting.
- And much more!

Made in the USA
Monee, IL
29 September 2023